Linda McGehee's
Simply Sensational
Bags

Linda McGehee

Published by

700 E. State St.
Iola, WI 54990-0001
Telephone 715-445-2214
www.krause.com

Please call or write for our free catalog. Our toll-free number to place an order or obtain a free catalog is 800-258-0929 or please use our regular business telephone 715-445-2214 for editorial comment and further information.

Library of Congress Catalog Number: 00-100067

ISBN: 0-87341-848-4

Printed in the United States of America

The following products or company names appear in this book:
Albe Creations, Inc., Alma Lynn, Armo® Fleece, Artemis Silk Ribbon, Baby Lock® USA, Benartex, Inc., Bernina of America, Inc., Brother® International Corp., Buttonhole Twist, Cache Junction Seitec, Cactus Punch Floral Dimensions, Candlelight®, Capitol Imports, Inc. of Tallahassee, Coats & Clark, Colorfast Printer Fabric™ Sheets, Cordonnet, Dritz®, Dyenamics Hand Dyed Fabrics, Elna USA, Fairfield Processing Corp., Fairfield Ultra-loft®, Fiber-Etch™, Fiskars®, Foundation by the Yard©, Ghee's®, gingher®, Gütermann of America, Inc., HeatnBond®, Hoffman California Fabrics, HTC-Handler Textile Corp., Jiffy Fuse™, JHB International®, Inc., John Kaldor®, June Taylor, Kreinik Mfg. Co. Inc., Little Quilts, Luny, Madeira™ Threads, mamamania-vintage buttons, Maywood Studio, Mettler® Threads, Moda Fabrics, Morning Glory, Mountain Mist/The Stearns Technical Textiles Co., P & B Fabrics, Pellon®, New Home Sewing Machine Co., Northcott-Monarch, OLFA®, Omnigrid®, PFAFF American Sales Corp., Polyfluff™, Quilters Only Springs Industries, Inc., Reflections™, Robert Kaufman Co., Inc., Schmetz, Singer, Staple Aids Sewing Corp., Starmaker 5™ tool by Kaye Wood, Steam-A-Seam 2®, Stitch Witchery®, Sulky® of America, The Snap Source™, Thermolam® Plus, Toray ultrasuede® (America), Inc., Transfer Fusing™, Tumble Dye™, Ultrasheen™, Viking Sewing Machines, Inc., The Warm Co., Wonder Under®, YKK® Zippers distributed by American & Efird Inc. in the U.S., YLI Corp.®.

Acknowledgments

Sewing is an adventure for me. A sewing machine is my vehicle. Thread and fabric are my fuel. Needles and feet are my tools. My friends in the industry who supply the products and equipment I use are my engine. I wish to thank those who have given me motivation while supplying their products and equipment.

I wish to thank those who have been involved by supplying products and equipment:

Sewing Machines and Accessories: Baby Lock USA, Bernina of America, Inc., Brother International Corp., Elna USA, The New Home Sewing Machine Co., PFAFF American Sales Corp., Singer, Viking Sewing Machines, Inc.

Batting, Fusibles, & Interfacing: Dritz, Fairfield Processing Corp., HTC-Handler Textile Corp., HeatnBond, Mountain Mist/The Stearns Technical Textiles Co., Morning Glory, Pellon, Staple Aids Sewing Corp., and The Warm Company.

Buttons: Albe Creations, Inc., JHB International, Inc., and mamamania-vintage buttons.

Cutting Equipment: Fiskars, gingher, OLFA, Omnigrid, and June Taylor, Inc.

Dyes: Cache Junction Seitec.

Fabrics: Benartex, Inc., Capitol Imports, Inc. of Tallahassee, Dyenamics Hand Dyed Fabrics, Hoffman California Fabrics, Maywood Studio, Moda Fabrics, Northcott-Monarch, P & B Fabrics, Robert Kaufman Co., Inc., Quilters Only Springs Industries, Inc., and Toray Ultrasuede (America), Inc.

Handbag Hardware: Ghee's.

Threads: Coats & Clark, Inc., Gutermann of America, Inc., Kreinik Mfg. Co. Inc., Madeira, Mettler Threads, Sulky of America, and YLI Corp.

Needles: Schmetz.

I am grateful to my students who have accepted my ideas and knowledge and asked for more; to the stores who continue to promote and sell my patterns, books, and other products; and to my colleagues in the industry who have enlightened me with questions and answers.

My utmost appreciation to those who supported me by entering the Ghee's Handbag Challenge.

My greatest appreciation to the designers who contributed their handbag creations.

Many thanks to Nancy at Ghee's who has proofed, manned the shop, and stood by me through hills and valleys.

My special thanks to Barbara, my editor, who patiently worked with me, and who made my puzzle pieces of photos and copy look absolutely wonderful in book form.

My very special thanks to my husband and sweetheart, Jack, who patiently proofed and pre-edited when I know there were other things he wanted to do, and wanted me to do.

My thanks to each of you for helping to make my life fun while enabling me to follow my dreams.

Table of Contents

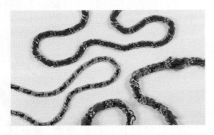

Foreword

By Karen Ancona, Editor CNA *magazine*

In this book you will have the pleasure of learning from expert fiber artist, teacher, author, and designer Linda McGehee. I have personally been in awe of Linda's talents for over a decade. She is one of those exceptional women who can create something useful and beautiful from a length of fabric, a hank of threads, and a bit of hardware.

Linda's talents go beyond making handbags and totes. But in the tome you currently hold in your hands, she concentrates on carryalls that are a part of the fashion world for women, children, and even men.

I have been visiting with Linda for years at trade shows that we both attend. The clothing she makes (and wears) stand as encouragement for everyone who ever wants to own or give something original and wonderful. Totally fascinated by one vest she wore with a matching handbag, I inquired, "Where did you find this lovely fabric?" She made it!

Linda lives the world of creative designer, always chic, always on the edge of something new. Linda has incorporated years of studying style and techniques into this book. Her explanations walk you through each style so that your end results will truly be as beautiful and as useful as what is shown in the lovely photographs. She encourages you to experiment with decoration, yet never leaves you without direction. Her purpose is to instruct, never to limit your own creativity.

Once you read this complete book, you'll never again search for that perfect bag or tote. You'll always know you can make your own — better, more suitable for your needs and that special outfit, than anything you can purchase ready-made. And after your first project, you'll agree that making a carryall is as easy as one, two, three. The only question you'll have is, "Now why haven't I been doing this for years?"

Introduction

My sister, Patricia and I spent many pleasurable hours mixing and matching garments to create the perfect fashionable outfit. That's me, the blonde on the right!

As a young girl, I was fascinated when I dressed up in my mother's clothes. My sister and I spent many pleasurable hours mixing and matching garments to create the perfect fashionable outfit. Shoes, of course, were oversize heels. Plastic pop beads became the most exquisite jewelry. The handbag always completed the ensemble.

Some of my first leather projects were handbags. In the '60s, with scraps of suede, I laced the pieces together to make them large enough to create a bag. One navy leather bag, I recall, made an excellent fashion statement. Another, with various shades of brown, would pass for a very nice hippie bag.

As time passed, I began to work with Ultrasuede, making garments for others. Having the experience of working with real leather, I was comfortable using the new fabric. My heart skipped a beat the day I decided to buy some for myself and I discovered the cost. From that day forward, I saved every morsel of Ultrasuede, knowing that it would have a use some time, some place. If my customer didn't want the leftovers, I would find a use for them. I don't think I have ever intentionally thrown away a scrap of Ultrasuede.

When I began teaching classes on Ultrasuede, my students wanted something to make from the larger leftover pieces. At this point I became more involved with bags. Cosmetic bags with zippers were lots of fun to make. The basic construction was simple, taking very little time to assemble. The size of the leftovers determined the decorative design. Although the project was small, it allowed me the creativity I enjoyed.

With time, I discovered the metal hardware used in ready-made handbags and found I could duplicate expensive ready-made handbags. It was then that my business turned to handbag patterns, frames, chains, magnetic snaps, feet, and hardware used to make bags. My palette, the handbag, gave me lots of creative freedom. I could fulfill my desire to design and sew, yet I didn't have to fit a body.

As you begin in this wonderful world of bag making, you will discover that constructing handbags requires some basic guidelines. Once you discover how easy it is to make them, there are endless possibilities. Create a bag for every season and social event. Make it basic or add creative manipulation of fabrics and decorations. The many extra touches to personalize a bag are endless. Consider a hidden pocket, strap variety, add a touch of handwork, and the list goes on.

You will have leftovers from garment construction, piecing, heirloom, or whatever. Use these leftovers to complete an ensemble in a creative way to show your individual personal touch. You can duplicate an expensive ready-made handbag at a fraction of the cost. Handbags are really simple to make and they can be such fun. The best part is you don't have to worry about fitting.

Over the years I have received many compliments on my bags. For some reason, others think you are so special when you can make a handbag. Maybe it is the hardware that looks so difficult, but really isn't. It is no different than sliding in a curtain rod. Perhaps the different shapes appear complex. For whatever reason you receive compliments, accept them with pride and make another bag. Bags are quite easy to make and they are a source of wonderful self esteem. May you have as much fun designing and creating handbags as I have.

Linda

A Little History

The lady's handbag is the counterpart of the man's pocket. It has gradually become an indispensable part of the female wardrobe. The material, shape, and size of the bag is dictated by frequent changes in fashion. Leading into another millennium, it is to be expected that the handbag will be called upon to meet a variety of new uses. Won't you need a practical handbag to securely carry the developing items of our technology?

Point of Interest

As in any venture, there are many tips and tricks that make stitching more efficient. Throughout the book, these hints of special interest are designated with this symbol to emphasize information, help speed sewing time, and guide you to professional results.

To give you a brief history of bags and names that were used in the beginning, here is an excerpt from *The Pictorial Encyclopedia of Fashion* (by Ludmila Kybalova, Olga Herbenova, Milena Lamarova, published in 1968 by Crown Publishers, Inc., New York).

Accessories are the innumerable unimportant and seemingly trivial features of fashion, which yet, taken together, indicate a style of clothing as much as the actual silhouette or colour. It is in this very toying with trifles that fashion expresses her insatiable desire for novelty. All through history we come across many a commodity which, though taken for granted today, once ranked among the most highly prized and highly priced adjuncts of fashion — the things 'one simply must have, my dear!' A history of accessories can therefore never hope to be exhaustive — the field is too wide. Every epoch created its own particular toys. From the 12th to the 17th century, for example, hand and pocket-mirrors were a favourite female adornment; they were worn on a gold chain around the neck, hung at the girdle, used as the centre of fans, framed in the tortoiseshell, ivory, or silvergilt, or combined with miniatures or etchings. The inexhaustible fund of ideas which we admire in the modern fashion industry was limited in those days to the medium of the craftsman's workshop. It is not until plate glass was invented and large wall-mirrors appeared that little mirrors were outmoded. An exhaustive history of accessories would have to include the vinaigrette, the pomander, the innumerable little caskets and phials, the toothpicks and the watches which all played their part in the image of a period.

DICTIONARY OF BAGS

Aumonière: From the French, 14th and 15th centuries. Worn by both men and women this leather coin bag was tied to the belt and was a forerunner of the pouch. It was later to be put to a variety of uses. It was an important and extravagant part of Burgundian court dress. Charlotte of Savoy, who died in 1483, left 23 elegant purses of white and red leather, velvet and satin.

Bandolier: An American Indian shoulder bag, usually a pouch made from buckskin and embroidered with beads. They were carried by women of the Great Plains Indian tribes, who kept combs, herbal cosmetics, and sewing things — for quick mends of the family's clothes — in them.

Backpack: A kind of knapsack, often attached to a lightweight frame, worn by campers or hikers. In the '90s, this common style handbag was used by kids for schoolbooks, as well as general carryalls for business or play. Often made of leather, denim, canvas, or tapestry, the style evenly distributed the weight over the back rather than one shoulder.

Belt: During the late Middle Ages a belt was worn to relieve the shoulders of the weight of the garment. A great deal of equipment could be attached to this belt: weapons, knives, pouches, and even bells. A purse hung from the belt was known as the aumonière.

Böurse: The French name for a purse or pochette used to carry cosmetics. The name also applied to the bag in which the hair was worn (circa 1730).

Carpetbag: An old fashioned traveler's bag made of carpet originating in the 19th century.

Handbag: A lady's handbag is the counterpart of the man's pocket. It is a small container for money, toilet articles, keys, etc. carried with or without a strap; a purse; a small case or satchel for use in traveling.

Kit: A soldier's equipment, exclusive of arms, now called a pack. Personal equipment, especially packed for travel or some particular activity or sport. Compact assembly of utensils in a container especially made to carry them. Basic sewing kit. I remember my father saying, "the whole kit and caboodle" but it never dawned on me what a kit was. Or what about the song: "Pack up your troubles in your old kit bag and smile, smile, smile."

Minaudière: A metal handbag for evening. Art Deco motifs with inlaid copper, brass, and German silver are lovely; others have gold-plated designs such as butterflies and are carried by woven gold chains. Garnet, lapis, carnelian, jade, onyx, rose quartz, and rhinestones are all used lavishly. Some are so beautiful they could be sculptures.

Miser Purse: A tubular, double-ended purse often netted or knitted, used by men and worn twisted through the belt.

Pocket: A fabric swatch sewed into clothing for carrying money and other small articles. Women's pockets in the 18th century consisted of a bag tied around the waist under the hoop. Since pockets were concealed until the early 20th century, there was a slit or opening in the dress to retrieve the pocket.

Pocketbook: A case or folder, usually of leather, divided into compartments, and suitable for carrying money, papers, and other personal effects. A small purse or handbag.

Pompadour: A drawstring bag of woven material usually velvet or lace used in the 18th century and named after Marquise de Pompadour, mistress of Louis XV.

Purse: A small bag, pouch, or case in which money is carried.

Reticule or Ridicule: A drawstring bag made of woven material on a long cord fashionable during the French Revolution. Well-to-do Victorian ladies had elaborate reticules to hold their sewing and other important supplies always at hand.

Shoulder bag: Originated as part of the WAC uniform in World War II.

Sporran: A purse or pouch hanging from the front of the belt worn by Scottish Highlanders in full dress, usually covered with fur or long hair and often ornamented with silver and stones.

Tote: A container or carryall, usually fabric, used to carry or haul in the arms or on the back.

THE MOST COMMON HANDBAG SHAPES

Are you confused about the styles of bags? Here are the most common handbag shapes from the National Handbag Association.

Chanel: Distinguished by quilt stitching and chain handles through eyelets.

Clutch: A small bag designed to be tucked under the arm, often features a detachable strap or handle.

Envelope: This style includes an Accordion or French (single) creased bottom with a flap opening.

Hobo: A very soft pouch-shaped bag with a shoulder strap and top zipper.

Satchel: A bag with a wide flat bottom and top handles.

Swagger: A pouch-shaped bag with outside pockets surrounding a center frame or zipper pocket with double handles or shoulder straps.

Chanel

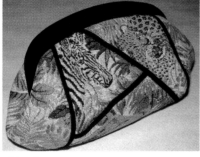

Clutch

Envelope

Hobo (on right)

Satchel

Swagger

CHAPTER 2

Building the Bag — The Under-Construction

ntil recently, there were few handbag patterns on the market. With the trends towards making accessories and small projects, handbag patterns have become more popular. Some of the handbags from Chapter 14 are actually patterns available on the market. The designers who have patterns to sell are listed in Resources at the back of the book. Their instructions may vary slightly depending on the style and type of handbag.

As in any pattern, the instructions should give explicit directions as to making that project. It never fails that there are always extra tips and tricks to make the pattern easier to construct. This book is designed to offer basic information on many types of handbags.

I use the handbag as a palette to show various types of embellishment. Sometimes this decoration may be complete before constructing the bag. Needlepoint, leftover quilt blocks, heirloom, and sequin fabric are examples. They are attached to the under-construction in the process of making the handbag. Other times the piecing may be stitched directly to the under-construction as in a stitch-and-flip method. Appliqué, decorative stitching, and other thread work may be applied directly through the stabilizer or under-construction to offer more durability.

There are no hard fast rules to follow in making handbags. Ideas may fluctuate as new products and styles evolve. Use this book as a basic guide to better understand the bag you choose to make.

A handbag requires a certain amount of under-construction to give stability and hold whatever is inside without stretching or distorting the fabric. Almost every bag needs something for support. The size and style of bag is an important factor and the weight and type of fabric chosen for the project will determine where to begin.

My first handbags were constructed of Ultrasuede, the synthetic suede with the fashion look of suede without the disadvantages. The fabric was stable, yet it needed a little more support to prevent wear and to hold its shape. After many experiments, I determined that Ultrasuede should be fused to another layer rather than stacking layers for weight. I chose fleece for the support layer.

Since I began working with Ultrasuede, I have made bags from every imaginable fabric. Some are very thick like tapestry and denim, others are very lightweight like silk douppioni, cotton, or lace. No matter how heavy or fragile the fabric may be, there are options in making a handbag. Don't be afraid to experiment before beginning your first bag. It's better to experiment now than to be sorry later when the bag is too soft for the style or too heavy to stitch.

There are a variety of fleece or needle-punch type products available on the market. Most stores hide these products, along with interfacing, somewhere under the counter. I guess they decided that since it's hidden in the project it should be hidden in the store. Be sure to ask, because fleece and interfacing are necessary in shaping a bag just like they are necessary to add crispness and shaping in a garment.

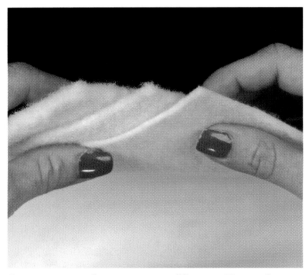

Companies produce a variety of fleeces. Choose the weight that is suitable for the style handbag you are making. Lighter fabrics require heavier fleece for support. More stable fabrics require lighter weight fleece.

The weight of the fleece you use is determined by the weight of the fabric. Many times a lightweight fabric may not seem practical for a handbag. To solve this problem, a lightweight fabric requires heavier fleece like Poly-fluff, Fairfield Ultra-loft, Armo Fleece, or Thermolam Plus. Sometimes it may be practical to use two layers of fleece or a layer of fabric and fleece together. Buckram is very stiff and suitable for bags but may or may not be the type of support you want. To determine a compatible weight of fleece, drape it and your fabric into a shape that resembles the handbag and check for the crispness and shaping you desire. Remember that fusing the fleece to the fabric will be slightly

crisper after fusing, but it will not add weight.

A heavy fabric like tapestry may require little or no support in a bag. Many tapestries have a rubberized backing that prevents the fabric from stretching. These may be stitched into a bag with no fleece. Others may be slightly lighter in weight and require only a layer of interfacing. Test a small piece while considering the style and size bag designed. Also consider the floating yarns in the tapestry. Some of them are extremely soft and shift easily.

In most cases, fusing the layers of fabric and fleece together produces the best weight. The layers are actually bonded together to become one, rather than two layers stacked together. One exception to the rule is knitting bags where batting is sandwiched between layers of fabric and machine quilted in fairly open designs. Stitch and flip is another exception. This is a strip piecing assembling technique used to combine strips of fabric on a base like batting or fleece where each strip is sewn on the base and flipped before an additional strip is added. Unless other instances arise, my favorite method to construct handbags is fusing fleece to the fabric.

Sandwich the fusing medium between the fleece and the wrong side of the fabric.

There are many fusing mediums used to hold layers of fabric together. Stitch Witchery, Jiffy Fuse, Steam-A-Seam 2, and HeatnBond are my favorites. These fusing agents are web-like bonding materials made from polyamide that hold two layers of fabric together without stitching. The web is placed between the two layers of fabric and dissolves into the fabric when heat, steam, and pressure are applied. When properly fused, the two become one. As products do vary and may be updated as new ideas arise, always follow the manufacturer's directions precisely and test before beginning a project with a new product.

Unlike interfacing, fusible webs cannot be used to stabilize an area to prevent stretching.

Be aware that fusible fleece is now available. When using this new fleece, it is not necessary to use fusible web. I keep both fusible fleece and several types of fleece in my studio. I never know when I am going to need it, so it's nice to have it close at hand.

Because I use certain fleece and interfacing on a regular basis, I purchase several yards at a time. In the long run it saves me a trip to the store at odd hours. I feel I save by stacking pieces closer together on the larger piece, rather than purchasing the yardage listed on the pattern and wasting part of it because it is not large enough to do anything else with.

Shapes of bags may vary according to styles, however the basic components are basically the same. Cut two pieces each of the fabric, fleece, and fusible web. To insure that the web is not larger than the fleece, I like to stack the layers together and cut them at the same time. This saves me a cutting step and I am assured that the fusible web is not too large.

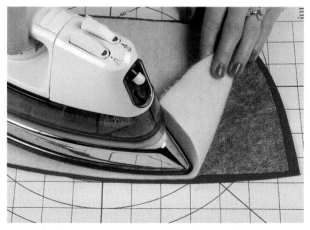

Fuse the layers together by using the wool setting on a good steam iron.

You will notice that the fleece in the photo is trimmed 1/4" (the seam allowance) smaller than the fabric to eliminate bulk in the seam allow-ance. When working with a lightweight fabric, include the seam allowance of the fleece for added stability and weight.

To begin constructing a bag, sandwich the fusible web between the fleece and fabric. Fuse the layers together by using the wool setting on a good steam iron. Most irons today produce quantities of steam necessary for good fusing. If, by chance your iron does not steam well, use a damp press cloth for added steam. Some fleece is sensitive to heat. Be certain the iron isn't set so high it scorches the fleece or fabric.

Once fused to the backing, the fabric becomes stable enough to construct a bag or ready for embellishment. The fleece acts as a stabilizer. The fabric will not shrink or stretch.

Rules to Remember

- *Handbags are the only item of apparel carried day in and day out, so quality is of utmost importance for the basic bag.*
- *Never make a bag any larger than you are willing to carry fully loaded.*
- *Use a chain on smaller bags.*
- *Use a strap on day bags.*
- *Large women look best carrying large bags and small women look best with small bags. It's amazing how many women overlook this basic rule of pleasing proportion.*
- *In the new millennium women will be categorized more by their attitude than by their age. Your attitude can be revealed and displayed by the handbag you carry.*

TROUBLESHOOTING

Separating a fused area. A fused area can be separated by re-pressing with steam until the fabric can be gently pulled apart. To re-fuse, insert a new piece of fusible web. Work quickly while the fabric is warm.

Removing fusibles from the iron. It never fails that fusible web touches the iron. Use a fabric softener sheet from the clothes dryer to wipe the fusible from the iron. This is a good recycling tip, too. Use an iron cleaner when the fusible web has been on the iron so long that it turns brown.

Removing fusibles from the right side of the fabric. If you leave bits of fusible web on the ironing board, they are sure to end up fused to the iron or fabric side of your project. The iron with fusible web on it is sure to touch the right side of the fabric. To remove the fusible web from an area, use a cotton ball to apply rubbing alcohol to the spot. Allow it to sit a few seconds to loosen from the fabric and scrape the fusible web from the fabric with your fingernail. If the alcohol has loosened the fusible web on the wrong side of the fabric, let it evaporate before re-fusing for the best bond.

Point of Interest

* *Determine the weight of fleece to use by the weight of the fabric and size of the bag.*
* *Fuse a heavy fleece to lightweight fabrics for added support.*
* *Fuse a lightweight fleece to heavy fabrics to avoid too much bulk.*
* *A large bag will require more fleece for shaping than a smaller bag.*
* *Proper fusing requires a combination of heat, steam, and pressure.*

CHAPTER 3

Decorating the Fabric

Decorating a handbag is the most fun of all. Because the project is small, it doesn't require a tremendous amount of one technique. The design may be simple and take very little time to construct or it may be very elaborate and take days to complete. The choice is yours.

Time is valuable. Many times I underestimate how long it will take me to finish something. I disappoint myself when I don't have the time to complete a project for that evening or last minute gift. When time is of the essence, let the fabric become the embellishment. Choose a fabric that stands alone and a handbag design that is quick to put together. Most handbag patterns should go together in a couple of hours. Consider the available time for the project and design accordingly.

EASIEST

When I am on a tight time schedule I like to allow the fabric to become the design. Many

Tapestry and laminated fabric are two fabrics that stand alone and look beautiful with no extra decoration.

brocades, faille, and other bridal or evening fabrics make an excellent choice for small special occasion bags. Tapestry and laminated fabric are two fabrics that stand alone and look beautiful with no extra decoration. A contrasting fabric like Ultrasuede for tapestries or chintz with laminated fabric offer the contrast in fabric texture and color for the strap, corded piping, and opening area. This subtle bit of variation distinguishes different areas of the bag and adds character to an otherwise plain bag. It is an effective use of fabric to offer a classic look, yet stay within a time frame.

Occasionally I find laminated fabric on the bolt but more often I find fabric I wish I could laminate to add water-resistant protection. Now I can, with HeatnBond, which offers two types of iron-on flexible vinyl. Choose the look you want with either luster or matte finish. This clear lustrous iron-on protection for fabric is designed to press to any smooth material for water-resistant clear protection. The adhesive formulation for quick and easy laminating uses the medium setting on a dry iron. The combination of dry heat and pressure makes it easy to

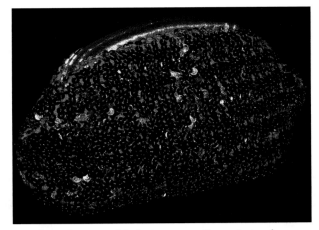

Purchased sequin fabric is an excellent choice for a quick evening bag.

laminate any flat fabric. Laminated fabric is a great choice for light-colored summer fabrics.

Always consider the durability in the areas that are handled the most. The strap and opening area receive the most wear and tear. Be sure the fabric you choose for the trim can handle the stress. Ultrasuede and drapery weight chintz are my two favorites. They are available in a list of solid colors, making them practical and easy to find.

Tapestry combined with Ultrasuede and denim make practical, easy to construct day bags.

QUICK STITCHING

There are a multitude of opportunities to stitch on fabric. Simple straight stitching offers many combinations without mentioning the decorative stitches from the machine. Let's concentrate on straight stitching ideas.

Use a see-through ruler and chalk marker to draw stitching lines on the right side of the fabric.

Use a see-through ruler and chalk wheel marker to draw a stitching line on the right side of the fabric in a pleasing manner. Choose a corner or center point to begin the first marking and continue to add lines by laying an increment from the ruler on top of a previous mark. This is the easiest way to make perfectly parallel lines using a combination of widths or the same marking. The advantage of using the chalk marker is that the chalk can be brushed off easily to correct a marking error.

The diagrams on page 18 show some of my favorite styles of straight stitch designs.

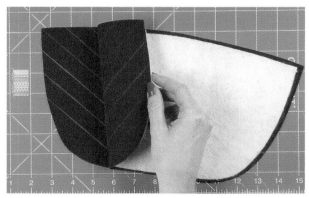

To draw identical lines on the front and back of a bag, first mark one side with a chalk marker. Lay the other side right sides together, and pat lightly with your hand. The excess chalk goes to the other side of the fabric, making a perfect mirror image.

It is difficult to mark both the front and back of the bag identically. The ruler may slip or each side could be started at a slightly different angle, causing the progression of lines to gradually grow apart. To make a mirror image on both sides, first mark one side with a chalk marker. Lay the other side, right sides together, pat lightly with your hands, and the excess chalk goes to the other side of the fabric. Oh how simple it can be to mark matching designs. If the lines are not quite dark enough, re-marking is an easy task.

Once the lines are marked, select a thread that matches or add color with several threads. An all-purpose thread may be too lightweight for embellishment. The thread imbeds into the nap of Ultrasuede, losing any signs of added workmanship. It is better to use a slightly off color so the stitching shows. For instance, on black use charcoal colored thread. I once made a peach bag using orange thread embellishment. Because the thread was so lightweight, the orange added a subtle design. Always lay some thread from the spool on the fabric to test. A full spool of thread never looks the same as a few strands of the thread away from the spool. When stitching through fabric and fleece with all-purpose thread, use a size 90 needle.

Use a charcoal colored thread on black for a subtle accent. Black thread would never show.

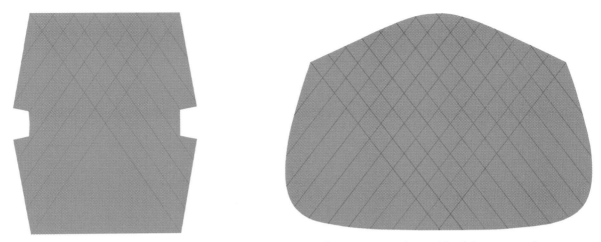

Diamond shapes spaced 1" or 1-1/4" apart, depending on the size of the bag. Use the width of the presser foot as a guide for perfectly straight parallel stitching. Change needle positions for varying widths.

Spaced 1/4", 1/2", and 1" apart in a square, plaid, or diamond shape; 1/2", 3/4", and 1" apart is another nice combination.

Diamond or square shaped lines spaced 1/4" and 1" apart.

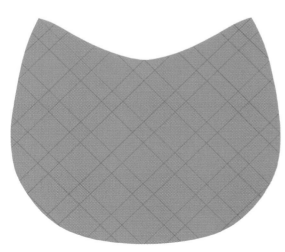

Diamond or square shaped lines spaced 1/2" and 1" apart.

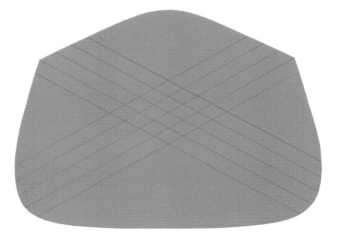

Lines are 1/2" apart.

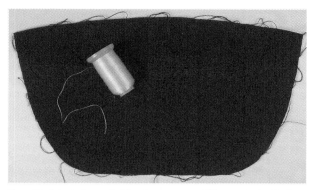

Topstitching thread, Cordonnet, and Buttonhole Twist are heavier threads that offer more visibility in decorative stitching. They are used in the needle of the sewing machine.

Topstitching thread, Cordonnet, and Buttonhole Twist are heavier threads that offer more visibility in decorative stitching. For best results, use a topstitching needle size 90 to avoid fraying the thread as it is stitched. The eye of the needle is designed longer and larger to accommodate the heavier thread. Longer stitch length makes for a prettier stitch. Too short a stitch will cause buildup of stitches and could perforate the fabric. A 3 length or longer allows the thread to stay on top of the fabric, showing more design.

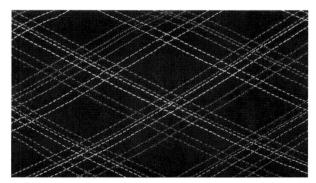

Use the width of the presser foot as a guide to sew perfectly parallel lines. Change the needle position for variety of stitching widths.

Another opportunity for play is a double or triple needle. Use a size 80 or larger needle. There will be options of distance between the needles from 2.0, 2.5, 3.0, 4.0, and 6.0. The distance between the rows of stitching will determine which needle is suitable for the project. Experiment on a fabric before starting the project. Note that stitching with a double needle on heavy fabric will not cause the ridge or pintuck like

lightweight fabric. The lines are simply parallel. A slight bump may be created when using a double needle that is spaced apart. Shortening the stitch length will cause a slight ridge.

Use a double needle to sew two perfectly parallel rows of stitching. On lightweight fabrics, the double needle may produce a ridge or pintuck.

The triple needle is another option for design.

Do some stitch variations and keep the tests in a booklet or in the back of this book for future reference. Label your samples with thread type and needle. A live sample is always better than photos.

Another of my favorite thread techniques is couching. There are numerous heavier threads designed for the serger that can be laid on the fabric and stitched over to hold in place. A single thread or several twisted together add texture and color to any fabric. Use my book *Creating Texture With Textiles* as a reference for other thread work. Refer to the chapter on thread, as well as sewing machine feet to produce quick, easy, and very artistic designs with the sewing machine. These heavier threads make a better showing than do needle threads. A variety of each in one project is well worth the effort.

As you continue sorting through thread for embellishment, you will realize that the options are more varied than ever before. There is an assortment of metallic threads available from every company. Add to that the lamé threads with a wonderful reflective quality, threads that glow in the dark, threads that change color in the sun, and probably more by the time you read this. It is phenomenal what is happening with thread today. This is one of the reasons it's much more fun to sew now than it ever has been.

No matter what type of thread you are using for emphasis and design, be certain to use the proper needle. Using the right needle determines whether the thread breaks or sews smoothly, whether the stitch quality is poor or the best, and whether you enjoy what you are doing or not.

To determine which needle is appropriate with which fabric or thread, consider these points. Choose the needle size according to the weight of the fabric. A #60 works best with lightweight fabric, #80 is designed for medium weight fabric, and #100 and larger penetrates heavier fabrics with the best results.

Use the correct point of the needle for the type fabric. For instance, a ball point spreads the fibers of a knit, avoiding making tiny holes in the fabric. A sharp needle pierces micro fibers to avoid skipped stitches. Many needles are slight ball point or Universal.

When working with decorative threads, the most important feature of the needle is the eye. Embroidery needles are designed with a slightly larger eye to accommodate rayon threads. The metafil needle has an even larger eye for work with metallic threads. The largest eye needle available is the topstitching needle. Because the eye is so large, the smallest size topstitching needle available is size #80. This is the needle I use for almost all of my decorative work. I am constantly changing from one thread type to another. The topstitching needle works best with each of these threads as well as two threads through one needle. To avoid changing needles every time I change thread type, the topstitching needle is my favorite to keep in the machine most of the time.

There are numerous heavier threads designed for the serger that can be laid on the fabric and stitched over to hold in place. Known as couching, these threads can be easily applied with feet to produce quick, easy, and very artistic designs with the sewing machine.

STRIP PIECING

If you are interested in piecing and have never pieced before, this is the perfect opportunity to experiment. Cut the shape of the fleece slightly larger than the pattern suggests. Because most fabric that you use for piecing is lightweight, you may need extra support in the bag. Fuse a layer of fabric to the fleece. This fabric will never be seen, so it really doesn't matter what color it is. I like to use leftover fabric from another completed project or a fabric I purchased and I'm not quite sure why I bought it. A layer of muslin would also work for added bulk.

I like to cut strips in obviously different widths when I strip piece. If I am inaccurate in cutting and sewing, it's not as obvious as it would be when cutting the same width strips. Use the stitch and flip method (see page 12) to completely cover the fleece. Once the entire fleece is covered, use the pattern rather than the marking to cut the bag shape. The marking is simply a guide. It is easy for the bulk of the fleece to cause shifting as each strip is sewn on. With lots of narrow strips sewn to the fleece, the piece may shrink slightly or shift.

One of my favorite piecing ideas uses stripes or plaids. When cut on the crosswise grain, lengthwise grain, bias, and sewn back together, the fabric takes on an entirely different appearance.

This strip-pieced silk douppioni, with its reflective quality, makes a truly original bag.

The straight lines of the handbag pattern offer a palette for many piecing ideas.

LOG CABIN

An easy traditional piecing concept for hand-bags is the log cabin and variations of the log cabin. Blocks may be constructed separately, stitched together, and applied to the fleece once they are large enough. This is also a good choice when experimenting with new blocks. You are only obligated to make a small portion of a quilt rather than the full quilt.

Log cabin is a perfect way to use a leftover block from another quilting project. If the single block isn't big enough for the pattern, add extra strips to make it large enough.

Another option is to stitch directly on the fleece in a stitch and flip method (see page 12). A variation of the log cabin begins with a triangle rather than a square placed at the top of the fleece. A strip is added to each side of the triangle in a stitch and flip manner until the fleece is entirely covered. Start with fleece slightly larger than the finished size bag. On a one-piece pattern that folds at the bottom rather than on a seam, the piecing continues and the front and back are different. On one side the strips slant up, angling the same as the triangle. On the other side the strips slope down. There is nothing wrong with this. Each side of the bag has its own personality.

Basic strip piecing or variations of the log cabin created from silk, Ultrasuede, and cotton.

The same shape bag gives the illusion of several patterns. One uses the arch with framework, and the other folds over to make a clutch. Each is suitable for piecing or thread work.

Red, white, and black come together in a variety of shapes, techniques, and designs.

WEAVING

Weaving has surfaced in my life every few years. Each time was a little different, yet each type of weaving is perfect for a bag. One of the first crafts I explored was making pot holders. The loops were aligned next to each other on a square frame with hooks around the outside edge. The loops on the cross section formed the length grain. The remaining loops were woven under and over the first loop to form the cross-grain of the pot holder. This is a very simple process that has several applications.

My next venture included weaving on a loom to make fabric and belts. Depending on the types of fibers used, the fabric could make a wonderful bag. I progressed to weaving strips of leather cut from scraps given to me. Woven into a larger piece, these scraps became suitable to make my hippie bag in the '60s.

Weaving ripped strips of fabric became my next adventure. For this technique, place a piece of fusible interfacing slightly larger than the finished size desired on a padded board with the pebble side up. Lay the strips very close to each other, touching but not overlapping. Choose to make the weaving lines vertical and horizontal at right angles to each other or begin at an angle to form diamond shapes. Use color and width variety in a pleasing manner, remembering that another strip will be woven with each strip. Use pins to keep the strips taut.

Weaving ripped strips of fabric creates interesting texture. Add decorative stitching with lamé or metallic thread for more interest.

Once the weaving process begins, weave under and over through the strips, keeping them tight with pins as each strip is added. Push rows close together to prevent holes from forming. When an area is finished, fuse to the interfacing to hold the strips permanently. Once the weaving is complete, fuse the entire piece, pressing from the top and bottom with plenty of steam. For further embellishment, add decorative stitching in metallic or lamé threads. This will stabilize the fabric for projects that have wear and tear. Trim to the desired size once the fusing and decoration are complete.

My latest attempt with weaving began with a large piece of Ultrasuede cut 1/2" larger on all sides than the pattern piece. Cut lengthwise strips or slashes almost but not completely through the ends. Make the strips symmetric or uneven parallel designs. I like the wavy line approach for special effect.

Cut lengthwise strips or slashes in Ultrasuede to begin the weaving process. I like the wavy line approach for special effects.

Pin a piece of fusible interfacing slightly larger than the suede to a padded board with the fusible side up. Place the suede right side up on top of the fusible interfacing so the wrong side of the suede is next to the pebble (fusible) side of the interfacing.

For the crosswise strips, choose a variety of colors or one. Ultrasuede has a nap, so suede cut in different directions will show color variety. This subtle color change adds appealing texture to a traditional design.

Apply a paper-backed fusing medium to the wrong side of all strips to bond the layers together later.

Use a paper-backed fusing medium like Wonder Under or Transfer Fusing on the wrong side of all the strips to bond the layers together later. I generally use scraps. It's easier to apply fusing to larger pieces than it is to apply it to narrow strips. The permanent fusing will take place later once the strips are woven into place.

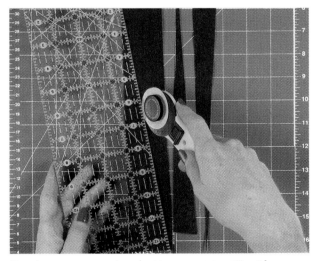

For the wavy weaving design, cut strips 1" wide on one end and angle the strip to 1/4" on the other end.

Cut straight strips slightly longer than the width of the base piece. These strips could be the same width or several widths varying from 1/4" to 1". For the wavy design, cut strips wide (1") on one end and narrow (1/4") on the other. It is important that the strips be cut straight so they

lay flush to each other once woven. Strips that are wide on one end and narrow on the other give the illusion of wavy lines in both directions once woven, although it is not the case.

Weave the cross strips under and over the length strips using the pot holder technique.

Give the ends a tug to keep them taut.

Using the pot holder technique, weave under and over through the long slashes, leaving the ends to extend on the sides. Give the ends a tug to keep them taut. Push rows close together to prevent holes from forming. Pinning is necessary.

After weaving several rows, steam the suede to the interfacing using a press cloth. Ultrasuede is very sensitive to heat. Without the pressing cloth there is a possibility of scorching. This pressing keeps the weaving in place and prevents slipping as future rows are added.

After weaving the full piece, steam the front carefully with a press cloth. Remove the pins and steam from the back to secure the design in its permanent position. Trim to fit the pattern.

A small section of the bag may be woven for special interest. Narrow strips of Ultrasuede cover the ends. Use the wavy rotary cutter and keyhole punch to add texture. Add couching for additional design.

Ultrasuede embellished with couching, weaving, and topstitching thread.

Appliqué

Basic satin stitch or 3-D appliqué is a perfect choice for a handbag. The color variety of Ultrasuede is excellent for trim on pillow ticking or denim.

Purchased lace or embroidery appliqués are excellent options for dressing up a special occasion bag or evening bag. Use clear monofilament thread to zigzag stitch the appliqué. Study the design and stitch in areas to hold the appliqué in place so the stitching becomes a part of the design. Many times I have seen such large stitches used to apply the trim that it looks like a spider web is holding a slapped-on appliqué. A little extra time and effort will make a difference.

Basic satin stitch appliqué on pillow ticking is a winning combination.

Stitch around the edges of the design using clear monofilament thread. Study the design so that the stitching blends into the appliqué rather than overpowering it.

Purchased embroidery, lace, or appliqué accents basic fabrics like moiré taffeta and handkerchief linen.

Sometimes the appliqué requires additions to complete the look. You can purchase lace trim by the yard. The rows of 1/4" ribbon shown in the photo at right were attached using the open toe foot, a double needle, and rayon thread using the feather stitch. Be sure the stitch doesn't swing so wide that it touches the foot, breaking the needle. Always test by hand walking the foot through the stitch before beginning to stitch.

The strips are actually pieces of fabric rather than ribbon, but either will do. When working with fabric, attach a fusible to the wrong side before cutting the strips. Cut the strips in different widths for variety. Use the edgestitching foot and a decorative satin stitch to attach to the base fabric. There is no need to worry about the raw edge, since the stitching predominately covers the edge. The fusible acts as extra security too. For the bag shown at right, I machine stitched on buttons collected from my button box to fill in the gaps. Notice the color combinations. The variegated thread doesn't match the fabric strips or the buttons, yet it all ties together in a pleasing manner.

The lace trim needed extra pizzazz. The 1/4" ribbon attached with a double needle, rayon thread, and the feather stitch combined to make the black-on-black evening bag.

Strips of fabric or ribbon are fused to the base fabric using a crossed or over-lapped design. They are stitched in place with variegated thread using a decorative stitch. The raw edges are covered with the decorative stitching, leaving no bulk. Collected buttons fill in the gaps.

HEIRLOOM

French hand sewing by machine or heirloom sewing is one of the most popular types of sewing today. There is always enough lace and embroidery left from making the garment to construct a bag to match. Consider this the opportunity to make a bag from scratch too.

This combination will make a nice hobo-style bag.

Use a combination of pintucked fabric, insertion, edging, and plaid fabric cut on the bias and straight to construct a hobo style bag.

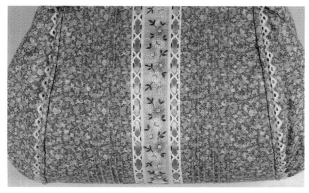

A small piece of leftover handloom may be inserted between rows of beading and pintucks to make a very simple, yet feminine bag.

Even an 8" strip of handloom may be inserted between rows of beading and pintucks to form the panel of a very simple bag. Assemble the bag with lace edging between the corded piping and side panel to tie the pieces together.

Stitch rows of lace and insertion together until the piece is large enough to make a small handbag.

Rows of lace or embroidery insertion and beading may be stitched together until they are large enough to make a bag. To attach flat, straight edges of val lace (a narrow, dainty, flat lace with fine floral design on a diamond shaped netting) together, butt the edges together and zigzag over the heading of the laces using a medium to narrow zigzag (1.5 to 2 width and length) and the edgestitching or joining foot. The zigzag width should be wide enough to cover the heading of the lace yet not too wide to close the lace. The zigzag length should be short enough to hold the laces together yet not as tight as a satin stitch (machines and laces vary). Spray starch laces for added body and ease of sewing. Match lace patterns where necessary or combine a variety of patterns. Use fine embroidery thread and a size 65 or 70 needle for heirloom sewing. Switch to all-purpose thread and a size 80 needle for construction of the bag.

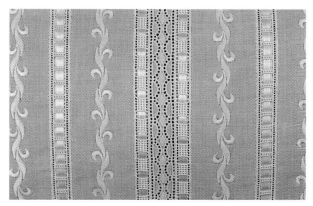

Placing the lace over a black linen makes the embroidery design more dominant and visible.

An additional step is necessary when working with embroidery lace. Using the edgestitching foot, zigzag over the edge of the batiste to roll the edge. Once rolled, butt the rolled edge with the beading and zigzag the edges together. Adjust the width and length of the stitch to match the size of the holes in the beading so that the needle stitches in each beading hole, leaving holes clean and open. Just as with val lace, use a fine embroidery thread and a size 65 or 70 needle for the lace work. The lightweight thread enables the lace components to blend together. The thread is not obvious or showy. The smaller needle stitches into the holes easily without grabbing more than it should.

Whether combining laces or embroidery, each has a transparent quality. Choose a fabric base in a pleasing color to fuse to the fleece. Overlay the lace on top. The background fabric is more subdued once layered. Test by laying the lace piece on several fabrics, either solid or figured, before cutting and fusing. Sometimes white or ecru is the perfect choice. Other times a color is best.

With embroidery machines and card designs so popular, it's easy to create your own embroidery trims or laces and duplicate some of the intricate handlooms of the past, which are so hard to find nowadays. It's not necessary to make a large piece for the central design. Also consider angling the pieces together rather than sewing straight strips. Variety is the spice of life.

Several rows of embroidery handloom, beading, and insertion form the panel in the center of a bag. The handloom is trimmed narrower at the top to shape the bag from a wider bottom.

Ideas using heirloom sewing for little girls through ladies styles.

A variety of styles and shapes of handbags are conducive to heirloom sewing.

ADDED TOUCHES

There are many tools designed for specific jobs that can be used for artistic additions other than the original purpose. Two of my favorite tools are the keyhole and buttonhole cutters. I detest making buttonholes but I love these tools to make decorative holes and slits for decoration.

Hand-woven fabric may be wonderful for a bag, but some styles of bags require a more stable fabric by the opening. Ultrasuede solves the problem, yet could use a little more pizzazz. Use the keyhole punch to make holes along the edge of the suede before applying it to the hand woven.

I used to very accurately and painstakingly measure with a ruler the position of each hole until one day it dawned on me that the holes in the edging of computer paper were perfectly spaced and a lot less trouble. Other times I decided it didn't matter if the holes were spaced perfectly so I eliminated some frustrations by just making holes in the fabric. The choice is yours.

Use the buttonhole cutter to make perfectly even slashes through which a ribbon, trim, or another piece of suede may be woven.

Rotary cutters are available in several wavy or pinking shapes to cut strips with a design rather than straight. Once you begin playing with these tools in this manner, you will be surprised at how many ideas evolve. Scraps become prized pieces.

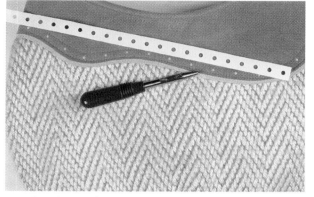

Use the edging of computer paper to perfectly align holes in the fabric. Ultrasuede combines well with hand-woven fabric.

The keyhole punch and wavy rotary cutter offer opportunities for design and play.

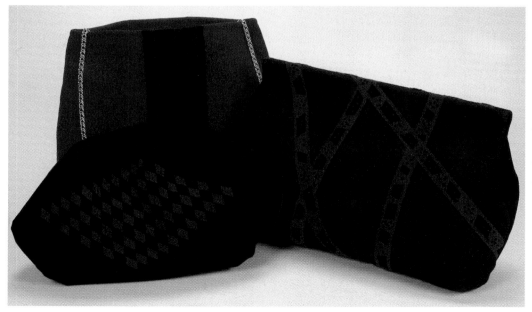

Scalloping shears, double needle, weaving, and sewing room tools used in combinations make experimenting with scraps lots of fun.

Combinations to Enlarge

I have received many pieces of handwork as gifts that were slightly too small for a bag. My walls are full and I didn't want to use them for pillows, so my thoughts returned back to bags. Use cross stitch, needlepoint, crewel work, silk ribbon embroidery, and other handwork as the dominate feature and fill in the rest with a fabric and trim that ties the work together.

The charted needlework in the photo is wide enough for a center panel but not quite long enough to go to the bottom seam. The design needs to be centered higher on the bag because of the shape and bottom seam. Burgundy corded piping ties the beige fabric to the denim and frames the needlework as if that's the way it was intended. Besides, the denim is more durable for the bottom construction.

A charted needlework center panel.

The handbag is the perfect place to showcase cross stitch, charted needlework, free-motion embroidery, and other small pieces of handwork.

A rug-hooking pillow design as the center panel.

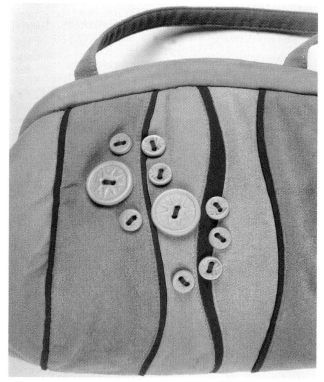

Scraps of purple Ultrasuede joined to make a piece large enough to make a bag.

The Little Quilts rug hooking pillow design shown above is slightly smaller than the center panel of a handbag pattern. To fill in, I used a larger corded piping to balance the thickness of the rug. The suede and hooking are both very compatible and durable for a bag.

I have been on a purple kick for quite some time. I have plenty of purple scraps of suede, yet none of them were large enough to complete a bag from one color. Since a raw edge of suede is a finished edge, it doesn't need to be turned under to prevent raveling. By overlapping and combining several different shades of purple, I built a piece large enough to make the bag. It looks as though this was planned from scratch, though it really is planned from scraps. The buttons stitched with darker thread tie the fabrics together.

Leather

Leather and suede are available in many weights, styles, and colors. Real leather is any animal skin that has been treated or tanned — kidskin, chamois, reptile, calfskin, and buckskin. Suede is a type of leather that has been buffed to create a napped surface. Unlike synthetic suede, which is sold by the yard and can be treated like fabric, real leather and suede are sold by the skin. For the best results, select a pattern design with simple lines that will highlight the leather. Avoid styles that require extensive easing because leather doesn't ease well.

Leathers crease easily, so it's best to roll them in a tube until ready to use. Because stitching marks leave permanent holes in leather, letting out seams or restitching can be disastrous.

Check leathers for irregularities and holes before cutting. For suede, use a "with nap" layout. Smooth and heavy buckskin types have no nap or bias to consider so a "without nap" layout can be used. It is best to lay out major pattern pieces in the lengthwise direction of the skin for greater stability. Although leather has no grain, it does have greater crosswise stretch. Small pieces can be laid in any direction. Cut a single layer at a time, holding pattern pieces in place with weights. Remember to turn pattern pieces over to cut the opposite side where necessary. Use very sharp shears or a rotary cutter.

Since seams are a focal point, especially on leather, your sewing machine must be clean and set up correctly. For best results, use a wedge-point or leather needle in the size appropriate for the weight of the skin. Hold seam allowances together with paper clips since pins will leave permanent holes. Use 8 to 10 stitches per inch and test the pressure on the pressure foot. It may have to be reduced since leather is thicker and spongier than fabric. Stitch slowly, taking care not to pull or stretch the leather. Do not backtack as it might tear the skin, but do knot thread ends securely.

To avoid stretching and for lightweight leather and suede, interface with an iron-on interfacing. Iron-on interfacing requires dry heat and neither leather nor suede reacts well to steam. Add interfacing using a warm dry iron with brown paper serving as a press cloth. Topstitch seams to flatten.

Some leathers and suedes spot easily, so avoid getting them wet. If they do get wet, allow them to dry away from direct heat. Wipe smooth leathers first with a soft cloth. Suede can be brushed when dry to restore the nap. Store leather handbags in a cool spot and cover with cloth, never plastic, to prevent the leather from drying out.

Leather and suede are available in many weights, styles, and colors. It is so easy to handle when making a handbag.

And More

As you explore this wonderful world of embellishing bags, let your imagination run wild. Experiment with the stitches on your machine using decorative or topstitching thread. The fabric can be as simple as pillow ticking or denim. Combine unusual techniques, textures, and colors. Build leftovers until they are large enough to use and add character to a handbag. I like color and plenty of it. I also like subtle and elegant.

Combine barzello with decorative stitching on crinkled fabric.

Experiment with decorative stitches on the machine. Use rayon thread for close satin stitch designs. Topstitching thread works best with more open stitches.

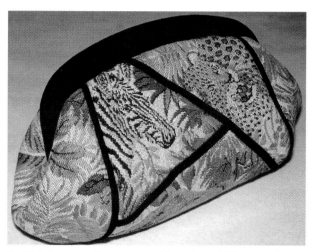

Build leftovers of tapestry with strips of Ultrasuede until the fabric is large enough to construct a bag.

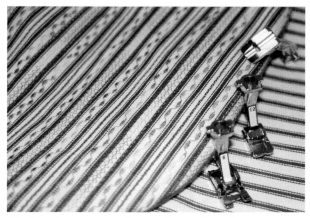

The blank stripe in pillow ticking offers the opportunity to show off decorative stitches and brighten the fabric with thread.

Basic black evening bags using double needle, beads, and couching.

Pockets

The lady's handbag is the counterpart of the man's pocket. Its purpose is to hold personal and utility effects that are necessary and used on a daily basis. It stands to reason that every handbag should contain a variety of pockets to facilitate maximum organization.

As the creator of the handbag, you can build the bag to suit your own personal needs. The bag should be functional. It should provide the ultimate in convenience. Think about the things you now carry in your bag. Include the things you *like* to have handy plus the things you *have* to have handy and things that every

Choose a variety of pockets to accommodate your needs. An open pocket on one side and a zipper pocket on the other eliminates confusion when filing necessities.

now and then you *wish* you had handy (like a small penlight). Plan a special place for each of these. Also allow a special place to remain empty just waiting for that impulse item that you will chance upon.

Decide on a size that is practical for your needs. Never make a bag larger than you are willing to carry when full. No matter what the size, mine always seems to be full. If there is a place for the essentials and everything is in its place, articles should be easy to find. An oversize bag could cause more trouble than it's worth.

Too many zipper pockets on one handbag could become very confusing unless they are labeled. Therefore, even though I always have a variety of pockets in my handbag, I never place more than one zipper pocket on the outside, especially if it is the same size and shape as another pocket. Otherwise, I am constantly fumbling to find what I hid where.

There are a variety of types of pockets to choose from when making a handbag and they may be applied to a variety of styles of bags. Determine the style of bag, what it is to be used for, and then choose the types of pockets that are suitable for that bag. A day or all-purpose bag will have different requirements than an evening bag.

OUTSIDE PATCH POCKET

The difference between a patch pocket on a garment and a patch pocket on a handbag is the stabilizing construction. A pocket needs the durability to hold the weight of keys and other articles thrown inside it. I like to bond the lining to the outside fabric. There may be instances where a layer of interfacing is necessary when lightweight fabrics are used. I find the parts of ready-made bags that fall apart the quickest are the pockets and lining, so they do require extra attention.

To make a basic patch pocket, cut two squares or rectangles slightly larger than the finished pocket size desired. One fabric should be the lining and the other the outside fabric. Allow for seam allowances on all sides. It's easier to trim off than it is to add on. If you're not certain of the size, always start bigger.

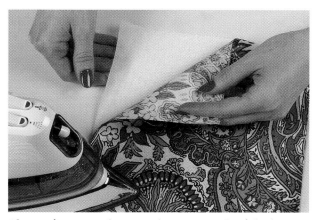

Place a fusing medium on the wrong side of the lining.

With right sides of outside fabric and lining together, stitch a 1/4" seam allowance across the top edge of the pocket.

With right sides together, stitch a 1/4" seam allowance along the top edge of the pocket. Place a fusing medium on the wrong side of the lining (see page 12). Pull the paper backing from the lining. Remember to keep the iron away from the fusing medium once the protective paper is removed to avoid getting the fusing on the iron.

There are two possible ways to finish the top edge of the pocket. The outside fabric may extend to the top of the pocket or the lining may be exposed slightly for added decoration. To make the outside fabric end at the top, finger press along the seam allowance so that the seam allowance ends at the fold. Press with an iron, beginning at the seam allowance and continuing to the three cut edges. The wrong sides are fused together to become one. Edgestitch or topstitch along the seamed edge with matching or contrasting thread to reinforce the pocket.

Fold the lining up and over the seam allowance, allowing the lining to show 1/4" as trim.

Stitch in the ditch, edgestitch, or topstitch to secure the upper edge of the pocket.

The other option allows the lining to show. Lay the outside fabric so it is flat, including the seam allowance. Fold the lining up and over the seam allowance, keeping the lining taut. Press the layers wrong sides together beginning at the seam allowance. Stitch in the ditch or edge-stitch along the seam line to strengthen.

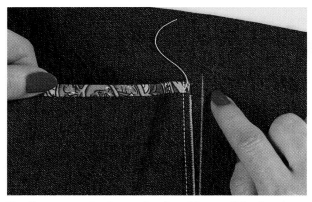

To allow space in the pocket for objects, slide the upper edges of the pocket slightly towards the center.

The side cut edges of patch pockets may be covered with straps to save bulk. The bottom cut edge will be encased in the seam allowance. Rather than placing the pocket flat on the side of the bag, slide the top edge toward the center 1/8" to 1/4", depending on the size of the pocket. This small amount provides space to put things in the pocket as well as to slide your hand in the pocket without ripping the upper corners. Once the bag is complete, the small amount of easing is not noticeable.

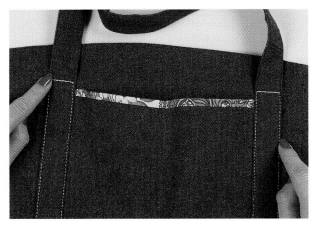

Apply the strap over the cut edges of the pocket. Triple stitch across the strap to secure the area where there is the most strain.

To apply the straps over the cut edges of the pocket, match the bottom edges, the front and back of the bag, to be sure the straps are aligned. Begin stitching at the bottom and edge-stitch 1/4" past the pocket opening. Come across to the other edge of the strap, backtack, and come across again before continuing to the bottom of the bag. This extra security stitching is important in this area where there is a lot of stress.

Another option with an outside patch pocket is to make the pocket almost the entire size of the bag. The bag may be left open, as one big pocket, or stitched into sections to accommodate special needs like a pen or notepad.

Make the outside patch pocket the full width of the bag. Stitch the pocket into sections to accommodate special needs.

The outside pocket may be covered with a flap for looks as well as security.

INSIDE PATCH POCKET

A patch pocket on the inside of a bag could begin very much like a patch pocket on the outside. Generally I begin with a fabric twice the size of the desired pocket plus seam allowances and the width of the bag. I plan for the pocket to extend from one side of the bag to the other. True, this is a large pocket but it can be divided later.

Extend a large pocket from one side of the bag to the other. Divide the pocket into smaller sections with stitching to make the pocket practical for pen, keys, checkbook, business cards ...

Fold the fabric in half, wrong sides together, and stitch across, forming a tube open on both ends. Turn right sides out and press the seam allowance at the bottom. Position the pocket on the middle of the lining (if the pocket is too low, articles lose their visibility when they fall to the bottom of the bag). Include the ends in the side seams while constructing the lining. Stitch the bottom of the pocket to the lining.

One large pocket usually isn't very practical. Use stitching to divide the pocket into sections. Begin at the bottom and stitch to the top edge of the pocket, reinforcing with back stitches at the beginning and ending. I like to have two pockets for pens and one for business cards, checkbook, or keys. Make the pockets suitable for your needs.

On my very first handbag pattern I chose a pocket size that was practical for me. It was amazing to me how many people thought the pocket was too large. On the other hand, it also surprised me how many thought it was too small. The size of the pocket should be determined by what is carried in it. Don't make the pockets so deep on a large bag that your fingers can't reach the bottom.

Make the pockets functional to provide the ultimate in convenience. Have a place for everything to stay handy.

OUTSIDE ZIPPER POCKET

This is the easiest zipper you will ever put in. I like to use the serger application because it finishes the edges as I am sewing but you can do it with a sewing machine too. This pocket may be inserted in the center panel of a bag that has three sections on one side or the raw edges may be covered with straps like the patch pocket if you prefer.

Again, it is better to begin with a fabric that is too large and trim down. Cut one lining and one outside fabric. Place fusing medium between the wrong side of the lining fabric and the wrong side of the outside fabric (the right sides of each fabric will be exposed). Fuse the layers together, being careful not to touch the fusing medium with the iron.

This zipper technique features an exposed zipper. Determine whether to match the fabric to the zipper coil or use a contrasting color for special effect. Determine the zipper placement and cut across through all thicknesses. This cutting will probably be about 1-1/4" from the top. It's easier to work with a zipper that is too long than it is to work with a zipper that is the exact length because the larger serger presser foot interferes with the zipper slider and stop.

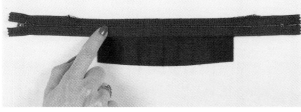

Place the right side of the closed zipper on the right side of the upper pocket. Serge or straight stitch the zipper to the pocket.

Place the right side of the closed zipper on the right side of the upper pocket, aligning the cut edge of the pocket with the zipper tape. Allow the zipper to extend beyond both sides of the pocket. With the zipper on top, serge the zipper to the pocket, trimming a minimum of fabric and zipper tape. With the variety of zippers available today, the amount trimmed will be determined by the size of the zipper tape.

Place the right side of the lower pocket on the right side of the zipper tape. Align the outside edges and serge the pocket and zipper as before.

Finger press the upper pocket away from the zipper coil. Place the right side of the lower pocket on the right side of the zipper, aligning the edges of the tape and pocket. The outside edges should match the upper portion of the pocket. Serge the pocket and zipper as before.

Finger press the pocket away from the zipper coil, making equal distance between the folded pocket and coil on each side. Using the edgestitching foot, stitch along the edge to keep the pocket flat.

Bar tack the ends of the zipper by the edge of the pocket, with the zipper opened halfway.

Finger press the pocket pieces away from the zipper coil. If by chance the exposed zipper tape is uneven, now is the time to correct that by folding the pocket fabric equal distance to the zipper coil. Edgestitch each side to hold the zipper flat using matching or contrasting thread.

Be certain the zipper is unzipped before trimming the extra tape from the pocket to avoid trimming the zipper slider off.

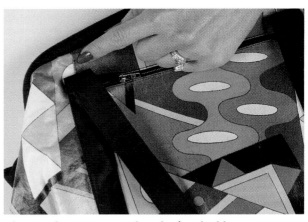

This stitching is exposed in the finished bag.

Pull the zipper slider to the center of the pocket. Bar tack each end of the zipper coil and trim off the excess zipper tape. Be certain the zipper is unzipped and the slider is within the pocket before trimming the excess zipper tape. It may be a good rule to try the zipper before trimming the excess. I was once in such a hurry that I trimmed the zipper slider with the tape, resulting in a permanently closed pocket. This technique is so quick and easy that you will probably do the same thing at least once until you get in the habit of testing the zipper before you trim.

Position the center of the pocket on the center of the bag. Trim the excess pocket if necessary. If

the pocket forms the center panel, stitch the pocket and bag layers to the side panels.

When the pocket is applied to a larger panel and the side edges of the pocket are encased under the strap, there is a slightly different approach. Fold under 1/4" at the upper side edge of the pocket to nothing at the zipper. Edgestitch the fold. This stitching is approximately 1-1/4" long. Baste the balance of the pocket to the outer fabric.

The strap covers the cut edge portion of the pocket eliminating bulk.

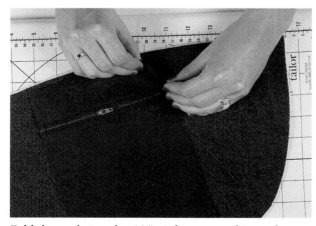

Fold the pocket under 1/4" at the upper edge on the narrow portion to nothing at the zipper edge. Edgestitch this section in position.

Beginning at the bottom edge of the pocket, position the strap over the pocket to cover the raw edge. Double check the positioning of the straps to be certain they match at the bottom of the other side. Secure the strap by edgestitching each side, beginning at the bottom and stitching 1/4" past the zipper coil to encase a portion of the fold-under. Double stitch the crossover from one side of the strap to the other for added security. This is the area of the straps that will bear the most strain.

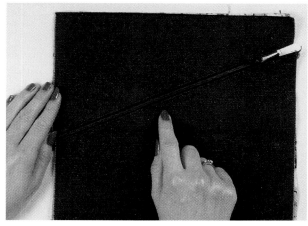

For variety, slant the zipper instead of making it straight across.

Feel free to experiment with positions of the zipper on the pocket. A slanted zipper is appropriate and offers variety.

INSIDE HANGING ZIPPER POCKET

I remember playing with a handbag that had a hanging pocket. This type of pocket is particularly clever in evening bags or large totes. Decide on the size of the pocket and double the

Place the right side of the zipper along the right side of the pocket width. Stitch the length of the zipper with a straight stitch or serger.

length and add 1". Add extra for seam allowances on the sides. The serger could be used to construct this pocket, however, this time the samples are straight stitched.

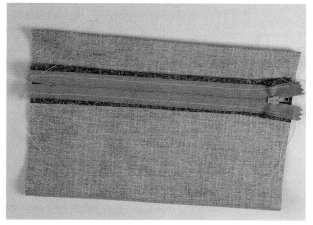

Fold the lower width of the pocket up to the zipper. Stitch in the same manner as the other end to form a tube.

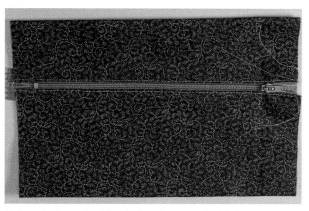

Edgestitch each side of the zipper to hold the seam allowance flat and prevent the seam allowance from catching in the zipper as it is zipped or unzipped.

Place the right side of the zipper along the right side of the pocket width. Using a zipper foot, stitch from the length of the zipper. Pull the other end of the pocket up to match the other side of the zipper tape. Turn the pocket right side out and edgestitch along both sides of the zipper coil to hold the seam allowance flat. This stitching prevents the seam allowance from catching in the zipper.

Turn the pocket wrong side out and fold so there is about 1" from the top fold to the zipper coil. Unzip the zipper partially and stitch the

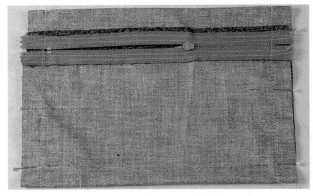

Turn the pocket wrong side out and fold so there is about 1" from the top fold to the zipper coil. Stitch the side seams with the zipper partially open.

side seams. The unzipped zipper becomes the opening for turning. If you fail to open the zipper, it becomes almost impossible to turn.

Sandwich the pocket between the lining and the casing while constructing the bag for a loose pocket on a small bag. Or stitch the folded edge of the pocket to the upper edge of a tote.

Insert the flap pocket between the casing and lining.

Secret Pocket

The secret pocket is a clever idea from Pat Lamb of Florida. The zipper pocket is placed in the bottom of the bag where it is concealed. This is a handy hiding spot for everyday or traveling. This idea works best with a pouch-shaped sectioned bag. The pocket becomes the width of the center panel. A zipper should be slightly longer than that panel.

Cut two pieces of lining fabric the width of the bottom seam by 6". For added padding, interface the lining fabric. Place the right side of the lining to the right side of the zipper. Sandwich the zipper between one pocket panel with the right side of the pocket panel next to the wrong side of the zipper. Stitch the length of the zipper using a zipper foot. Pull both layers of fabric away from the zipper and edgestitch to hold flat. Repeat the same process on the other side of the zipper.

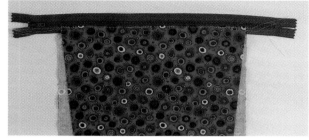

Sandwich the zipper between the lining and the pocket with right sides of the lining and zipper facing each other. Stitch and edgestitch both sides of the pocket to hold in place.

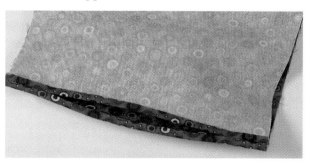

Matching the lower pocket pieces, stitch the seam allowance, leaving a hole for turning.

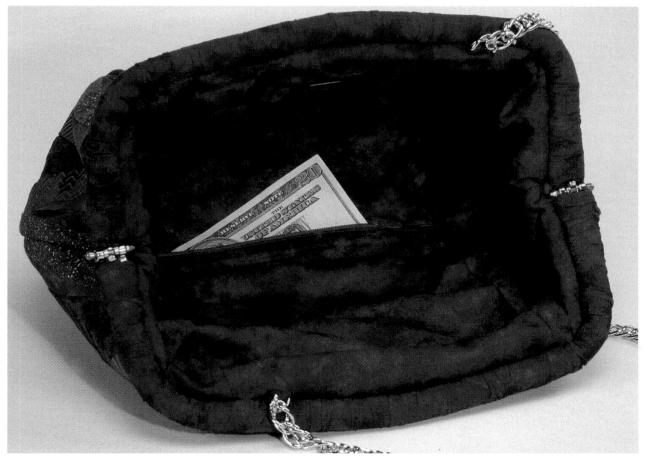

The zipper secret pocket is placed in the bottom of the bag where it is concealed from normal view.

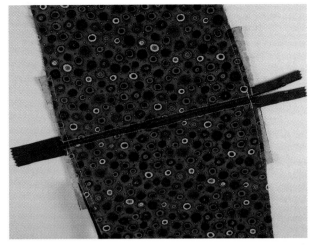

Position the hole in the pocket to match the zipper coil. Stitch a small seam allowance through two layers of pocket and one layer of lining to hold the layers together. Be certain the zipper is partially open.

Align the bottom edges of the pocket and stitch a seam allowance width approximately 1-1/4" on both sides, leaving an opening to turn the bag later. With the zipper closed, fold the pocket so that the opening for turning is under the zipper. There will be a tunnel under the zipper, forming the pocket. The zipper becomes the bottom seam. Unzip the zipper halfway and bar tack the zipper on both ends. Machine baste within the seam allowances to form the pocket.

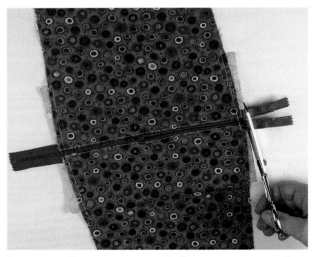

Be certain the zipper is open before cutting to avoid trimming the slider off.

Trim the excess pocket and zipper tape. *Be sure the zipper is open to avoid cutting the slider off.* Continue making the bag as though the secret pocket was not there.

POINT OF INTEREST

✦ *Choose pockets that are functional and provide the ultimate convenience.*

✦ *Never have two zipper pockets the same size on the outside of the bag.*

✦ *Stabilize the pockets for added durability.*

✦ *Divide a large patch pocket into smaller sections to accommodate special needs.*

✦ *Be certain the zipper is partially unzipped before trimming the excess tape away.*

✦ *For a finished look, use the serger to finish the seams of the zipper pocket.*

CHAPTER 5

Strap Variations

Unless you are making a clutch-style handbag, there will be some kind of strap or a chain used to carry the bag. I tend to make a strap for day bags and larger totes and use a chain or small cord for evening bags. Determine which is more practical for the bag you are making. Look through Chapter 14 (page 98) to see just a sampling of the unlimited possibilities to the use for a strap.

You can make a fabric strap in several different ways. You can braid the fabric, use a belt, weave yarn or suede through the chain, or slide a heavy cord inside the strap, to name a few. Choose the one that complements the look of the handbag you are about to finish and the one that is the most comfortable to carry.

FABRIC CHOICES FOR STRAPS

When I first began to make fabric handbags, strap making seemed very simple. I would stitch a tube of fabric and turn it. For very soft fabrics, this was a good solution, but it didn't work for every fabric. Besides, the lightweight fabrics were often too soft to make a durable strap for a handbag.

While working with tapestries, I discovered that such heavy fabrics were extremely difficult to turn from tubing. The construction of the fabric was too weighty, resulting in bulky lumps and bumps that looked very homemade. After playing with a variety of fabrics, I discovered various solutions, depending on the types of fabrics used in construction.

Insert bias corded piping plaid between the layers of strap to add interest.

To add interest and color variety to a solid colored bag, insert a contrasting color of bias binding in the side seams of the strap. Or use it to carry over the embellishment coloring to the strap. This has to be stitched and turned. Another alternative is to insert bias plaid for special effects. It is very subtle, but when the bias is available it makes a nice finish.

On an Ultrasuede strap, fold the outside edges to the center and fuse the layers.

One of my favorite ways to make straps began when I made lots of Ultrasuede belts for interchangeable belt buckles. To make an Ultrasuede strap, determine the finished width of the desired strap and double it. Interface the full width for stability. Position a fusing medium on the full width. Fold the outside edges to the center and fuse the layers, using the wool setting on a steam iron. If the cut edges slip during pressing, pinch them together while the fabric is warm. Topstitch along the edges for added strength and appearance.

Keep the cut edges flush for the most durable strap.

Add a bit of decoration to the strap by covering the cut edges with a strip of Ultrasuede trimmed with the wavy cutter to cover the cut edges.

The strap is finished at this point, but you can add more decoration by covering the cut edges with a narrow strip of contrasting color cut with a straight or wavy edge. Use the keyhole punch for more texture or decorative stitching. Have fun — experiment.

I often cover the raw edges of tapestries with Ultrasuede. It is so simple and much easier than turning tapestry. You'll need to decide whether to use combination tapestry/Ultrasuede as the top side, or just tapestry as the top of the strap. Ultrasuede has a grabbing quality, so it's especially handy on the underside of the strap to prevent the bag from slipping off the shoulder.

CUTTING THE FABRIC

Most woven fabrics have a slight give on the crosswise grain, whereas the length doesn't have much give. Whenever possible, I prefer to cut straps on the length of the fabric for stability. There may be occasions when lengthwise cutting is not possible and that's okay, but I prefer to cut on the length. As mentioned earlier, the crossgrain of Ultrasuede is the bias of the fabric, so the length doesn't stretch. As with woven fabric, it is my preference to cut Ultrasuede on the length too.

When you have to cut the strap on the crossgrain, interface the fabric with a fusible interfacing to prevent stretching during use. The weight of the interfacing is determined by the weight of the fabric. Most times I use knit interfacing cut on the length grain. Because I constantly make handbags, I have a 40" long piece of knit interfacing tucked away and labeled for straps. Whenever I need interfacing for a strap, I don't have to search for a long piece, I have a strip readily available. When the piece is used down to nothing, I begin with a new 40" piece. In the long run, this will save you money because there is absolutely no waste. It also saves time spent scrounging in the box or bag of tiny pieces that are never long enough.

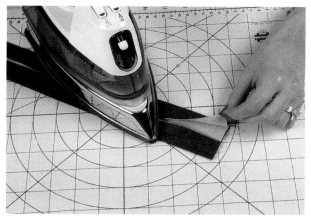

Fold the strap in half lengthwise and press. Open the strap and fold the cut edges wrong sides together to meet the fold.

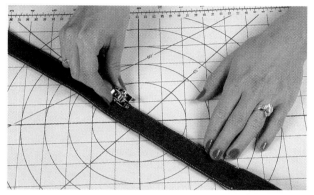

Fold the strap in half again and edgestitch the edges using an edgestitching foot. The strap is ready to insert into the bag or add to other hardware on the bag.

There is an easy way to make a fabric strap without having to turn the fabric inside out. Begin with a strip of fabric four times the desired width by the desired length plus seam allowances. Fold the fabric in half lengthwise and press. Open the strip and press the outside cut edges to the center fold. Fold in half along the original pressed fold line. Using the edgestitching foot aligned next to the open edge first, move the needle position to the desired distance from the fold, and stitch the open side closed. Stitch the remaining edge so that both edges are stitched evenly. For added decoration, it is sometimes nice to add several other rows of stitching.

INSERTING THE STRAP

On most bags, you will insert the strap between the outside fabric and the lining at the side seams. Another variation is to stitch the strap on the outside of the completed bag. First, stitch the end of the strap through all thicknesses by the upper portion of the side seam. Fold the strap up to cover the end of the strap and stitch across. Always double stitch a strap as there is more stress on a strap than any other section of the bag.

When a casing is used to hold a frame, another option is to sandwich the strap between the casing and outside fabric. Decide whether the ends of the strap should be placed on opposite diagonal sides for balance. Perhaps, in the instance where two straps are used, one strap is placed on one side of the bag and the other strap is placed on the other side.

The strap may be placed over a pocket to hide the raw edges of the pocket and add extra support for the weight of the bag.

Another alternative is to begin the strap at the bottom of the bag and continue stitching it up to the top. Leaving a determined amount of strap, finish stitching the strap down the same side as described in the Outside Patch Pocket (see page 42). This strap application can be used on bags with or without pockets.

USING CHAIN

Chain can be used with smaller style handbags or evening bags that are not heavy. The weight of larger bags on the chain could injure the shoulder or split the chain. Straps are stronger and distribute the weight of heavier bags.

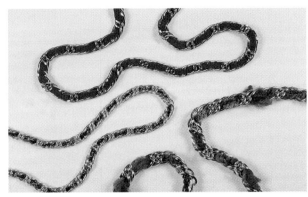

Weave suede, yarn, or ribbon through chain for added interest.

For decorative purposes it is interesting to weave suede or leather, yarn, or ribbon through the chain. The weaving process may shorten the chain length, so be certain to weave the chain before cutting the length. To shorten the chain, use wire cutters to cut a link of lightweight chain. For heavier chain, use two pairs of needle nose pliers to twist a link apart to separate the chains.

Slide a double split jump ring to the last link of the chain to make the chain link large enough to attach to the bag.

Many chains suitable for handbags have very small interlocking links. To attach the chain to the bag, add a double split jump ring to the last link. This tiny ring is a very small version of a key ring. It slides onto the chain link and slips round and round until it is secure on the chain.

Making the Fabric Loop

The jump ring is large enough to accommodate a fabric loop stitched to the bag. It is essential to use a fabric loop rather than just stitching for support to hold the weight of the bag. My favorite fabric loop is made like a belt loop or a miniature version of the strap. Begin with the fabric loop 1" by about 6". Because the fabric is so tiny, I prefer to make the strap longer than necessary just to have something to hold onto and because most of the time the beginning stitching isn't as pretty as I would like it to be. Since there is ample length, I can trim the ugly away. The 6" length is long enough to make a fabric loop for each end of the chain.

Slide the fabric loop through the double split jump ring.

Slip the fabric loop through the double split jump ring, leaving it longer at this point. To attach it to the handbag, stagger the ends rather than laying them on top of each other. This spreads the weight on the loops and avoids unnecessary bulk. When beginning to stitch,

To avoid unnecessary bulk, spread the weight of the fabric loop.

place the needle in the center of the loop, stitch forward and then backward to hold in place. If you begin at the edge of the loop, the loop generally slips from underneath the foot, making it necessary to start over.

The fabric loops may be stitched between the lining and the outer fabric.

The fabric loops may be stitched between the lining and outer fabric at the side seams, stitched under a facing as shown, or stitched between the casing and the lining.

✦ *Use a chain only for small handbags or evening bags. Use a strap on everyday bags and larger totes.*

✦ *Whenever possible, cut strap fabric on the length of the fabric.*

✦ *Interface the strap fabric for strength.*

✦ *To save time and money, keep a 40" long piece of interfacing tucked away and labeled for straps.*

✦ *Smaller bags require a narrower strap than larger handbags.*

✦ *Always double stitch a strap for durability.*

Corded Piping — A Detail Element

The final detail is always important to me. What good is a wonderful photo if the frame detracts from it? Why use matting if it takes away from the artwork or not use it if its absence leaves the design looking washed out or unfinished? Fine tuning the last detail will finish the bag so it looks professional. It makes the difference between haute couture and craft.

Corded piping is my number one favorite trim. There are so many opportunities with corded piping and each depends on what is included in the rest of the bag. There are two important factors to consider — design and bulk.

Corded piping adds a nice finishing touch of detail to handbags. Use contrasting colors and textures like Ultrasuede and denim for emphasis.

DESIGNING WITH CORDED PIPING

Study the fabrics and embellishments in the bag. What colors and textures will enhance the final appearance? A complete contrast may work best for a very subtle trim. Ask yourself questions and lay fabrics in between the sections to experiment. Will a little more metallic draw the sides to meet the front when the greatest portion of the decoration is metallic? What color is best to pull out shades in the piece? How large should the piping be? Is there a stripe or plaid fabric suitable for piping and how should that be treated?

Ultrasuede is one of my favorite trims. The bias is the crosswise grain and the lengthwise grain doesn't stretch. Though many believe this wonderful suede-like fabric is expensive, 1/4 yard cut into 1" strips for corded piping equals 11 yards. After checking your math and pricing other trims, I am sure you will discover that Ultrasuede is an inexpensive trim, plus it's very durable, doesn't ravel, is washable, and combines well with fabrics like tapestry, denim, and pillow ticking.

Many times, double corded piping is the proper finish. Choose two sizes of cord to work with. The size of the piping should be proportioned to the size of the bag. My favorites are 1/8" and 1/4" together. This will vary with each project, but it is a good general rule.

When making double corded piping, be certain to cut wider fabric strips for the larger piping.

When making double corded piping be certain to cut wider fabric strips of the larger piping. The smaller piping stacks on top of the larger piping seam allowance in construction. Though this fabric is not seen, it is necessary for layering the piping together. It is better to have a larger seam allowance in the piping and trim the excess away than to have a skimpy seam allowance. Don't cut yourself short.

Sometimes piecing is not wide enough to complete the bag. Corded piping will separate the piecing from the added fabric. In the photo the same size cording was used for both pipings. The red ties the minimal red coloring from the added fabric to the red in the piecing. The darker piping is a filler because it was needed for the best appearance. It is an optical illusion that the red piping is larger than the filler because it is brighter.

The red ties the minimal red coloring from the outside fabric to the red in the piecing.

A striped fabric for corded piping offers two possibilities — cut on the crossgrain or the bias. Since the stripe was pieced on the crossgrain, the corded piping is cut on the bias. Smaller bias corded piping offers better contrast than larger. The piping is an accent for the piecing, which is wider. This is another situation where layering the fabrics to test is of the utmost importance.

The narrow bias-cut green piping combines with the larger purple corded piping to offer the best contrast and detail.

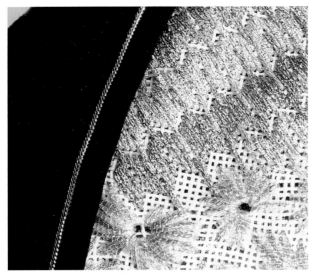

Purchased gold metallic corded piping emphasizes the metallic in the needlepoint handwork.

A small purchased gold metallic corded piping emphasizes the metallic in the needle-point handwork. By itself, the gold didn't show and just using the black took away from the handwork. The double corded piping has just the appeal to make the metallic stand out.

Embroidery edging combined with bias-cut plaid corded piping combines the contrasting elements.

One of the basic components of heirloom sewing is lace edging. This means that one side of the lace is straight and the other is scalloped or of a decorative design. Sandwich the straight edge of the lace or embroidery between the base fabric and add corded piping to extend the overall appeal of the lace.

Eliminating Bulk

Corded piping, whether purchased or made, is bulky. Whenever possible, remove as much of the unnecessary thickness as feasible. Many times on purchased piping, the cording is woven into the outside fabric or yarns, making it impossible to remove bulk. Depending on the construction of the bag, choose one of these two ways to insert the corded piping.

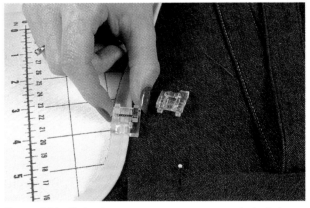

To avoid bulk in the cross seam, curve corded piping toward the cut edge of the seam it is being attached to about 1" before the cross seam. Stitch with the corded piping foot for more accuracy and ease.

Instead of using the zipper foot, use a piping foot to stitch corded piping. Slide the corded piping under the groove in the bottom of the foot. Move the needle position next to the cord to prevent slippage and to keep the cord snug in the piping. Refer to my book *Creating Texture With Textiles* for more detailed instructions on feet that make any sewing task easier.

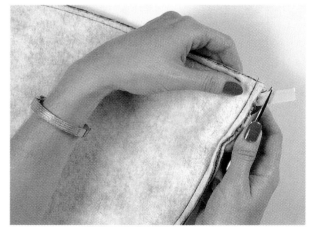

Remove extra bulk after the seams are finished.

The result is a smoother seam along the cross seam where a casing may be attached.

Pull the cord from the piping and cut the cord that extends into the seam allowance to eliminate bulk. Note the combinations of fabrics used in this project.

To avoid bulk in the cross seam, curve the corded piping towards the cut edge of the seam it is being attached to, about 1" before the cross seam. Add the next layer of fabric to encase the corded piping between the two seam allowances. Any excess may be trimmed. The result is a smoother seam along the cross seam where a casing may be attached.

The other alternative is to extend the corded piping into the cross seam. This process is the best procedure when the outside fabric is attached to a lining. To avoid bulk, pull the cord from the piping and cut the cord that extends into the seam allowance.

Sometimes corded piping should extend to the top of the outside fabric.

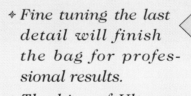
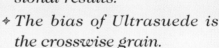

- *Fine tuning the last detail will finish the bag for professional results.*
- *The bias of Ultrasuede is the crosswise grain.*
- *Double corded piping is an excellent choice for final emphasis. Use metallic, stripes, plaids, or edging for more detail.*
- *Good sizes of cording are 1/8" and 1/4", depending on the size and design of the bag.*
- *Use the piping foot for best results when attaching corded piping.*
- *Change the needle position to stitch closer to the piping to maintain a snug fit.*

Building a Bag — Finishing Touches

The purpose of this book is to give practical information, tips, and short cuts that are not normally found in a pattern. There are patterns available for specific styles and shapes of handbags but much of the under-construction is pretty much the same. As with garment patterns, I like to change the embellishment, pockets, straps, and piping to suit my needs.

There are basically two types of bag construction. One uses a frame of some sort at the upper opening portion of the bag to hold the shape. The other has no framework for support but rather depends on the structure to keep the shape of the bag.

CHOOSING AND INSERTING THE LINING

The lining in the first nice leather handbag I purchased fell apart before the bag showed any signs of wear. For this reason, the fabric used to construct the lining is very important to me. My first handbags were made with the dyed-to-match fabric for Ultrasuede. These soft silky fabrics weren't suitable in weight and they scooted all over the cutting area and sewing machine, making them not so much fun to work with. To handle this problem, I decided to inter-face the lining with knit interfacing. The interfacing accomplished two things — it stabilized the lining, making it easier to work with, and it made the lining more durable for lasting wear.

After making several bags with beautiful linings, my students and friends started paying as much attention to the inside of the bag as the outside. I began to search for pretty or contrasting lining, whether it was suitable for the bag or not, because I knew I could stabilize it. The inside of the bag became just as exciting as the outside.

Many patterns give instructions in the cutting layouts for interfacing and lining even though they may be the same pattern piece. The easiest way to save time, a cutting step, and aggravation is to fuse the interfacing to the lining before cutting. This way, any shrinking will happen before the lining is cut and there won't be a problem of matching curves or corners because the lining is cut after it is fused.

My favorite interfacing is the fusible knit interfacing. It leaves the fabric stable, yet not stiff or cardboard like. No fusing pebbles show through the lining fabric as happens with other interfacings. I can't say it replaces all interfacings by any means, but it does meet my basic needs for many of the types of sewing I do.

There may be times when you want to make an unconstructed simple bag with no pattern.

Rather than make the outer fabric and the lining the same size, make the lining slightly smaller to accommodate the bulky layer between the two. The lining will always appear larger than the bag if the lining isn't cut smaller and takes too much space on the inside of the bag. To save yourself from cutting two pattern pieces, stitch the bag with a 1/4" seam allowance and the lining with a 3/8" seam allowance. On a larger bag the proportion will vary.

After fusing the interfacing to the lining, stitch the seam allowance, leaving an opening in the bottom for turning.

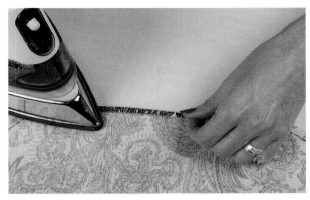

Press the seam allowance back for later ease of closing the opening.

Stitch any tucks or miters in the lining before attaching to the outside fabric.

After fusing the lining and attaching any pockets, stitch the outside curved seam or the side seams, depending on the style. Leave an opening in the bottom for turning. In the case of a fold at the bottom of the lining, leave the opening in the side seam. I like to machine baste the opening closed. Press the seam allowance back for later ease of closing the opening, and remove the basting stitches. Any tucks or miters can be stitched into the lining at this time.

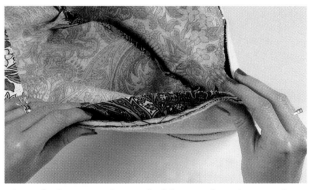

Place the lining and outside fabric right sides together and stitch the seam allowance.

Turn the lining right side out, leaving the outer fabric wrong side out. Place right sides together, matching any seams along the way. Stitch the seam allowance, holding the layers of lining and outer fabric together. Turn the bag through the opening in the bottom, add snaps or feet as needed, and close the opening using the edgestitching foot.

See how simple and fun it is to make bags?

CASINGS FOR HANDBAG FRAMES

For the handbags that use a frame to hold the shape by the opening, an extra strip of fabric is necessary between the outer fabric and the lining. Depending on the style of bag, this strip may be visible when the bag is closed or tucked inside the bag.

It's a good idea to stabilize the fabric strip with fusible interfacing or fusible fleece to cushion the fabric around the frame. This fabric strip is called a casing. The frame will slide

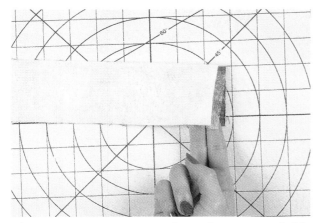

When a casing is incorporated into the pattern to hold a frame, fuse stabilizer to the outside fabric to cushion around the frame.

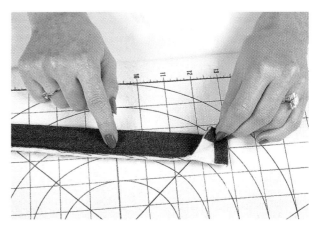

Fold the casing in half lengthwise, wrong sides together, and baste the length of the casing.

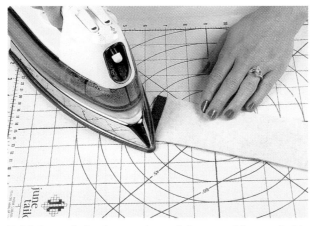

Fold the ends back over the stabilizer and fuse to hold in position.

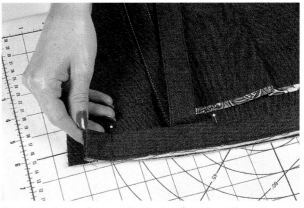

Position the casing on the body of the handbag, leaving space before the seam allowance to insert the frame.

through the casing much like a curtain rod passes through a casing or heading.

Fuse the fleece to the wrong side of the outer fabric, leaving a 1/2" strip of outer fabric on both ends to fold back onto the fleece. Use scraps of the fusing medium to fuse the 1/2" sections wrong sides together to the fleece. This fusing holds the fabric flat so that the frame, when passed through the casing, will not catch on the fold back.

Fold the casing in half lengthwise, *wrong sides together,* and machine baste the length within the 1/4" seam allowance. It's easier to baste the thick layers together than to pin the bulk. Because it's difficult to stitch an 1/8" seam allowance, use the width of the presser foot as a guide and move the needle position to the right.

Place equal amounts of fabric under the presser foot.

Position the casing on the body of the handbag, leaving space before the side seams. The casing has a finished edge which *should not* reach the side seams. Once the casing is sandwiched and stitched between the lining and outer fabric, the casing hangs free with an opening to slide the frame through on both ends. The bag is turned through the opening as before. There is no stitching around the frame. The frame is assembled after the stitching is complete. Before closing the lining in the bag, add a magnetic snap and feet if desired. It's that simple to finish a handbag with a frame.

CHAPTER 8

Big Totes

ig totes make it possible to carry an abundance of things, whether for travel, exercise class, school, sewing or quilting classes, knitting, diapers, or whatever. Remember the rule to never make a bag larger than you are willing to carry full. The weight in this tote could be tremendous.

I first began to make the totes in the photo using two place mats. They required no under-construction. It was the easiest bag I ever made. Fold over the fringe edge enough to form a casing for the frame and stitch the outer edge. These were featured in the book *Treasured Wrappings* as cosmetic cases. Each required one place mat. The embroidery was added for extra decoration. Trims, appliqué, or decorative stitching could be substituted.

These super simple totes were made with place mats.

Create double-faced quilted fabric by sandwiching fleece or batting between two layers of fabric. Choose crinkle and couching for quilting designs, or laminated fabric with wavy stitching.

Experiment with basic strip piecing and seminole patchwork on totes.

In transferring the same idea to fabric several opportunities arose. The easiest option other than using place mats is to use double-faced quilting fabric. This fabric seems to come and go in the fabric store and sometimes there is very little selection. I like to make my own double-faced quilted fabric by sandwiching batting between the wrong sides of two fabrics. The lining fabric becomes the folded edge at the top, so it is visible in the finished project. Pin or use a spray glue to temporarily hold these layers together to avoid slipping while stitching the quilting lines. When using a stripe, stitch the lines in the stripe. Draw an artistic pattern or straight lines on the layers and stitch with decorative thread. Choose heavier thread to couch for embellishment. Use two pillow blocks to build the tote. The palette is large enough to experiment with several ideas.

This is a chance to experiment with basic strip piecing. Spray glue the fleece to the wrong side of the lining fabric. This will temporarily hold the layers together while stitching. Start in the center and work outward. Place the right side of the first strip up along a diagonal starting line. Place the next strip on top of the first strip with right sides together. Keeping the cut edges even, stitch a 1/4" seam allowance. This stitching will show on the lining side. Turn the strip over to expose the right side. Press. Attach the next strip in the same manner, following the stitch/flip/press method until the fleece is completely covered. Trim the outer edges of excess fabric and complete the tote.

Use the narrow rolled edge on the serger to create the illusion of tiny corded piping between the rows of piecing. Add a narrow rolled edge ruffle or keep it simple with a wide tuck for detail.

This can be a serger or sewing machine project. Fold under the top edge to form a casing or add a tuck with contrasting color, cluny lace, or a ruffle created on the serger with a narrow rolled hem and differential feed. The fabric and recipient determine the final detail. The options are unlimited.

While attending classes with Mary Ellen Hopkins, the author of *It's Okay to Sit On My Quilt,* the students made smaller quilts or wall hangings to learn specific patchwork designs. By the end of the week we each had five to ten tops for quilts. Mine were the perfect size to make totes.

As with any large tote, the small things fall to the bottom and become lost in the shuffle. This tote idea can be reduced to a small cosmetic size. Make a very long belt loop and attach the two together at the upper edge seam allowance. It makes it easy to keep track of things.

Big totes are the type of project where the available fabric determines what size the finished tote will be. There are no hard and fast rules and the project can be made as easy or as difficult as you choose.

Make it easy to keep track of the small things. Attach one end of a long belt loop to the upper edge of a small clutch and the other end to the big tote.

Optional Hardware for the Professional Finish

There are a variety of metal closures and fixtures that are easily attainable to use in the handbag for a professional finish. They may be easily inserted into the bag using a pair of needle nose pliers. I recommend keeping a pair of pliers with your sewing equipment to avoid a trip to the garage or toolbox where the dirty tools are.

MAGNETIC SNAPS

When you look at ready-to-wear handbags, you will often see magnetic snaps used to hold flaps in place as well as to close the handbags. The snaps are purchased in a set with a male and female part and two metal support pieces.

Determine where the snap should be placed on the handbag. Position the prongs on the

A magnetic snap secures the opening of the bag, making it look like professional ready-made bags.

back of the snap on the right side of the fabric. Push the prongs into the fabric to mark the position. The prongs are generally not sharp enough to push through the fabric so you'll need to use very sharp pointed small scissors or the point of a button cutter set to cut a slash long enough for the prongs to slide through.

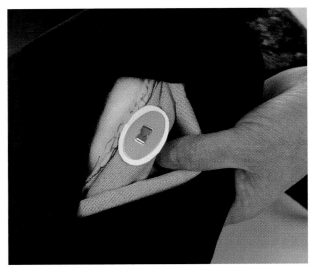

Push the prongs of the snap through the fabric. To prevent the metal support piece from cutting the fabric, place a piece of lightweight plastic or cardboard between the lining and the metal support piece.

To prevent the metal support piece of the magnetic snap set from cutting the fabric, place a piece of lightweight plastic from a clean milk jug or a piece of lightweight cardboard from a soda carton over the metal prongs on the wrong side of the fabric. This plastic or cardboard support piece should be slightly larger than the metal support piece. Slide the metal support piece over the cardboard. Use pliers to bend the prongs flat over the metal support piece. Be certain the prongs are flat so they won't puncture the lining or bag later.

FRAMES ENCASED WITHIN THE BAG

The metal frames used in ready-made bags are purchased in a pair. One end has three prongs and the other end has a single prong. The prongs fit together like a door hinge except the center prong acts like a spring to hold the bag open or closed. To line up the holes in the prongs requires a little pressure. Use pliers to hold these layers together and get better leverage.

The metal frames used in ready-made bags are purchased in a pair. One end has three prongs and the other end has a single prong.

Align the ends just like a door hinge. Slide the rivet in the first two holes.

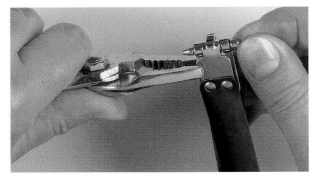

Use pliers to hold these layers together and get better leverage.

Working with two holes at a time, slide the rivet into the first two holes. The third hole will be far out of line. Using the pliers, press the ends together to align the holes. Slide the rivet through the final hole to secure the frame. The frame will stay open or closed.

HANDBAG FEET

To keep the base of day bags clean, use handbag feet designed for that purpose.

Position the feet according to the style of the bag. Some bags are rounded and others are flat.

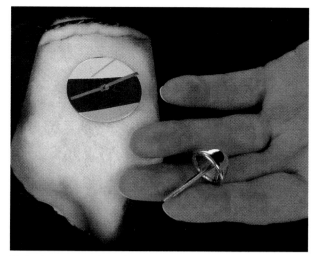

Slide the point of the foot through the bottom of the bag. Use a support piece of cardboard or plastic to stabilize and spread the prongs on the backside.

Day bags made with tapestry or suede generally have a flat bottom and it's easy to get the bottom dirty with normal wear and tear. To keep the base clean, use handbag feet designed for this purpose. They are purchased in a set of four. Position the feet in the location where they will give the most support. Coming through the hole in the bottom of the lining, use the keyhole punch to make a hole through the base of the bag in the proper positions. Use a support piece of plastic or cardboard like you did with the magnetic snap. Beginning on the right side of the fabric, slide the point of the foot through the hole in the bag and the support piece. Use pliers to spread the prongs on the backside.

When all accessories are in place, close the opening in the bottom of the lining with the edgestitching foot.

Linda's Favorite Collection

Of the many handbags I have made over the past 30-something years, there are certain special ones that are important to me. Here are a few of my favorites.

For my first invitation to the Fairfield Show, I decided to pay tribute to the area where I was living at the time and to my passion for making handbags. Being in New Orleans and knowing the excitement of costumes at balls and parades, I created something to fit that atmosphere. The purple, gold, and green ensemble that resulted represents the colors of Mardi Gras and incorporates many of the techniques I used in my book *Creating Textures With Textiles*. Glitzy textured threads, metallic piping, and dyed embroidery add to the mystique of crinkled velvet, lattice piecing, and couching. Nothing is too loud for the Carnival Season.

The inside of the "The Bag Lady Goes to Mardi Gras" coat showing a variety of handbags to carry with the ensemble from the prestigious Fairfield Fashion Show.

I couldn't decide on a final design for a matching handbag. Not knowing which bag to carry with the outfit, I made several which you can see on the inside of the coat. "The Bag Lady Goes to Mardi Gras" graced the cover of *Creating Texture With Textiles* and has appeared in several magazines. Unless you have seen the garment on the runway, you haven't a clue what the inside looks like. The model doesn't let the audience know until the finale. This is the first publication showing the collection of four bags on the inside. Composed of the leftovers from the coat and dress, mini lights, and sequin appliqué, there are variations to choose from stitched to the inside of the lining. The actual bag carried by the model used Sulky metallic in a double needle stitched in two directions to form diamond shapes for the side panel. The center panel used heavier metallic threads and yarns couched on cotton velveteen. This is a wonderful runway piece and it always creates quite a stir from the audience when the model shows the inside assortment of bags.

This bag was designed for a show Shirley Botsford curated at the Houston Quilt Market and Festival. Each designer received a box of goodies to work with.

The bag carried by the model was loaded with Mardi Gras beads to throw into the audience.

My box included Shirley's fabric, charms, buttons, cross locked beads, thread, braiding, cording tassels, and gold and silver rickrack.

Several years ago, Shirley Botsford asked me to participate in an accessory show she curated for the Houston Quilt Market and Festival. She designed the fabric and other companies contributed products to include in the projects. Charms, buttons, cross locked beads, thread, braiding, cording, tassels, gold and silver rickrack, and batting were among the items in the box that arrived. The bag pictured above evolved from that box of goodies.

McGehee is a Scottish name, derived from Clan MacGregor. With this Scottish blood coursing through my veins, you can understand why I like tartans. The MacGregor tartan is a favorite, but I'm not opposed to wearing others or combining several into one project. Note the use of the selvage where the authenticity of the tartan is stamped. This temporary writing removes with dry cleaning, but I used it as a focal point in the bag, planning never to clean the bag. Trimmed with Ultrasuede, the tartan collection bag grabs the attention of the audience at any Highland event.

The Royal Stewart tartan is one of the most popular tartans and it is repeated frequently in ready-to-wear garments, particularly at Christmas time. The darker portion of the tartan is centered high on the center panel as a focus point. Red and green double-corded piping accents and defines the center from the side panels, where the tartan is placed on grain. The same tartan has appeal on the straight grain or bias. The fold-over envelope bag is perfect with the bold stripe from the tartan centered. Bias would not be as effective.

Perhaps because of a bit of Scottish blood in my background, I enjoy working with tartans. There is so much opportunity to play with plaids on the straight of grain as well as the bias.

Combinations of bias and straight strips cut from the same tartan offer variation. For added texture, insert a raveled strip between the seams. Loosely woven fabric is easy to unravel or fringe by pulling a thread from side to side. Be certain to leave enough fabric on the raveled strip to stabilize for application into the seam. This is a combination appeal from only one fabric using the Black and White Scott tartan.

I have inherited buttons from many sources — my grandmother's collection, friends, and the remains from a closing store. To pay homage to buttons, I created these button bags. One is truly a collection from the button jar and the other is embellished with handmade buttons that tie the purple collection of fabrics together, making it appear as if this was the original plan. It actually evolved because I needed something to finish the bag.

Having never entered a challenge before and being nudged by a friend, I decided to submit a handbag made solely of the challenge fabric. Double-needle work and couching ribbons and threads on crinkled Hoffman fabric gave the illusion of several fabrics. The bag turned out quite glittery, with cross locked beads and rhinestones. The bag traveled the states for a year.

My entry in the Hoffman Challenge using only the challenge fabric, but adding ribbons, threads, beads, and more.

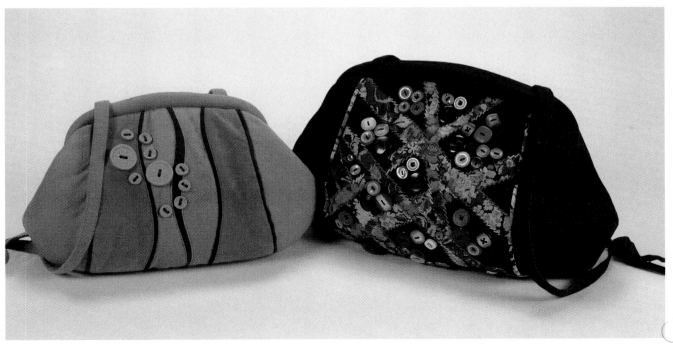

I enjoy watching projects evolve from using leftover fabrics and "things" found in the sewing room.

Using the smallest of scraps, smaller pieces than leftovers, from the cover garment of my very first book, I created this very elegant tiny bag. The simplicity of this handkerchief linen crinkled and couched bag combined with pintucking is perfect for the elegant garment. I love to combine contrasting ideas in one piece. With a separation of corded piping, the very straight rigid lines of the pintucks flow with the very crooked lines of beads and ribbons.

Leftovers from the front cover garment of my very first book.

Very rarely does one embellishment stand alone. I like combinations of color, technique, threads, and fabric.

My infatuation with daisies enticed me to design an embroidery disk for Cactus Punch, making very realistic dimensional flowers.

Very rarely does one embellishment stand alone. I like combinations of color, technique, and fabrics. Couching over piecing, accenting those with large corded piping and topping it all off with 3-D embroidery. Another possibility is combining several couching procedures with contrasting color on a base fabric like denim, highlighted with embroidery.

Never underestimate the power of basic black. This 3-D embroidery from my Cactus Punch Floral Dimensions disk is actually a detachable pin suitable for a hat, belt, or corsage. It never ceases to amaze me how so many ideas can be placed on one bag. This is an experiment with bypassing colors and allowing the nylon sparkle organza to show through the veins and outline stitching. It is time to play more with thread mixing and this idea.

Another of my favorite flowers is the poinsettia. Add a 3-D embroidery flower to any basic black handbag for more holiday appeal.

The opportunity to make patriotic handbags is limitless. From piecing to needlework, red, white, and blue are always a winning combination.

Nothing is more inspiring to me than seeing the American flag waving in the breeze. Combinations of techniques set the tone for the 4th of July purse shown in the photo above. The cross stitch pattern from Alma Lynn (upper left corner) highlights the pillow ticking with Ultrasuede trim. Charted needlework in shades of burgundy, beige, and navy rayon thread blend well with denim.

While learning to use my serger, particularly while trying to pick up speed on my new machine, I serged strips of fabric with wrong sides together, using a four-thread machine with basic cotton thread to create the bag shown in the upper right corner. I left the seam allowance and stitching exposed on the outside. I lifted the knife and folded the fabric across grain at different intervals and stitched again. I serged one row to the right and the next row to the left, creating a wavy design. By the time I finished the project, I was serging with the pedal to the metal!

The envelope bag uses a combination of two fabrics pieced into four log cabin blocks. The striped fabric cut on the bias added a nice contrasting trim.

The small bag in front offers a nice story and a lesson in creativity. At a quilt show, I purchased a packet of fabrics that I thought were fat quarters. Once home and opened, I discovered that they were fat eighths. There was no piece large enough for the upper edge without piecing. Rather than look like I stitched two pieces together, I cut them at a diagonal. I eliminated bulk in one spot and created the illusion of a planned design.

I've been attracted to bright vivid colors since Ann Boyce taught at one of my schools. Silver lamé and black seminole piecing combined with basic strip piecing using jewel tone cottons produced the most colorful tote. Many times a small portion of lamé, whether woven or knitted, adds a special sparkle. These fabrics require stabilization to handle any kind of wear. My favorite interfacing is the knit or tricot. It is strong, yet soft and not cardboard-y feeling. Cross locked beads and large jewels add to the glitz. This is one of those bags you carry when you don't mind attention, because it is a conversation piece. The red, white, and black smaller clutch version offers other color options when the jewel tones are too bright!

Use silver lamé, large jewels, and beads to add sparkle to any tote.

On days when you want attention, carry a tote pieced with bright colors and lamé.

Create a memory tote for grandmother using school pictures or candid photos on the Colorfast Printer Fabric Sheets. The pictures form the pockets on the rug tote. These are three of my grandchildren.

Create a memory tote for mom or grand-mother using school pictures or candid photos. This bag features three of my grandchildren and is a very quick project I designed for the book *Treasured Wrappings*. The basic bag is a light-weight rug with straps made from belting-by-the-yard. There is no under-construction.

Simply fold each fringed end right sides together 1". Stitch near the fringe to hold in place. The two fringed rug ends become the top (opening) of the bag. Fold the rug in half, matching the folded fringed ends.

Now that you know the size and shape of the tote, it's easy to determine the pocket place-ment. Mark the position for the pockets with pins or a marking pencil. Place the pockets above the midsection rather than towards the bottom. Once the tote is full, the bottom becomes wider than you think and it's better for the pockets to be positioned toward the top so the contents won't fall out.

Open the rug before stitching the pockets. To make the memory pockets using computer images, scan existing photos with a computer scanner. Or have your 35mm film developed on CD Rom and import to a document, or use a digital camera and import to a document. When you are satisfied with the image, print it on computer printer fabric, following the directions on the package.

If you don't have access to a computer, you can transfer photos to fabric with photo transfer paper. To be certain the photo is permanent, spray it with a fabric sealant. The clear matte finish protects the fabric design.

Note: Some computer printer fabric may not be permanent. Be certain the computer fabric you purchase is permanent and the design will not fade in the rain or washing. I used Colorfast Printer Fabric, a 100% cotton fabric that passes through color inkjet printers and copiers.

Enlarge the photo to pocket size and print on the printer fabric. Interface with fusible interfacing for extra durability. Position the photo right side down on the ironing board and place the pebble side of the interfacing down on the wrong side of the computer fabric. Fuse the layers using the wool setting on a steam iron.

It's that easy to print photos, drawings, or text. As printer fabric has evolved, there are several types of fabric or transfer paper available on the market. Be certain you have the Colorfast Printer Fabric Sheet because it will not lose the color with washing, liquid spills, or rain.

Fold under the top edge of each pocket and stitch to secure. Fold under and press the sides and bottom of each pocket. Position them on one side of the tote. Stitch in place to secure. For more design, stitch rickrack or other trim around each pocket. Another option is decorative stitches from your sewing machine.

POINT OF INTEREST

- *Search through your collection of odds and ends and choose several to use as a focal point in a bag.*
- *Tartans and plaids may be cut at different angles to create different points of interest.*
- *Use the serger for decorative stitches that show rather than utility stitches that don't show.*
- *When given lemons, make lemonade.*
- *Feel free to experiment with combinations of techniques. Layer several different methods together. Use contrasting textures.*
- *Any time a fragile fabric like lamé is incorporated into a bag, interface that fabric to stabilize. Always press from the wrong side and double check the heat setting. Most delicate fabrics use the wool setting or less.*
- *Use a lightweight rug or place mats as a quick project tote. Make them in minutes.*

Quick and Easy Bag Projects

Besides being useful to the creator, small, quick, and easy projects make excellent gifts. They are also a perfect opportunity to experiment with techniques, new tools, or products without going overboard spending lots of time and money. The cosmetic bag, the sweater/lingerie bag, and the shoe tote fall into this category of fun, fast, and useful projects.

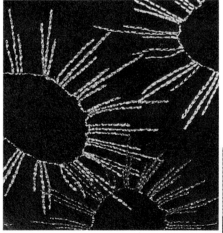

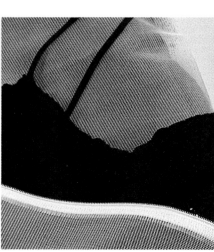

COSMETIC BAG

Don't hide your cosmetic bag inside a big tote. Use these tiny bags as great looking and affordable evening clutches and take them out on the town.

Ultrasuede is one of my favorite fabrics to work with. It doesn't create a lot of lint in the sewing machine, making it a clean fabric to work with. Because it doesn't ravel, a cut edge is a finished edge. And even the tiniest pieces can be useful.

I like to use scraps to make decorative designs. When I play with tools in a manner different than their original purpose, my creative juices just run wild. For those of you who say, "I'm not creative," just begin with something — anything — and discover what possibilities happen.

You will need:

+ 9" x 12" piece of Ultrasuede
+ Scraps of Ultrasuede, ribbon, or other trims
+ 9" x 12" plastic from shower curtain or picnic tablecloth (vinyl may be purchased by the yard)
+ Thread to match and for decoration
+ 7" zipper to match or contrast
+ Basting glue

Instructions:

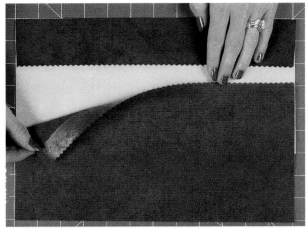

Combine long narrow pieces together to create the width necessary for the project.

1 For some reason I seem to have a lot of long, narrow pieces of Ultrasuede in my collection. If you do too, you can build these until they are large enough to make the 9" x 12" piece. Use basting glue to hold the layers together until they are stitched. The glue works far better to prevent slippage than pins.

2 Fold the 9" x 12" piece of Ultrasuede in half to make a piece 9" x 6". This is the area to decorate. The zipper will later be attached in the fold.

3 Before trimming or cutting any shapes from the scraps of Ultrasuede, apply a fusing medium to the wrong side. My favorite for appliqué or trimming is Steam-A-Seam 2 because of its double-stick quality. Apply the fusing medium to the wrong side before cutting new shapes. This saves a cutting step, prevents getting fusible on the iron, and makes appliqué easier.

Even the tiniest pieces become useful for creative design.

4 Cut different shapes of Ultrasuede with scissors, pinking shears, or a wavy cutter from a rotary cutting set. Position the shapes in a pleasing design on the 9" x 6" Ultrasuede piece. With the Steam-A-Seam 2 the design will stay in position until fused permanently. Other fusibles may shift if picked up or bumped.

Use the wavy rotary cutter and keyhole punch to enhance tiny strips for more character and creativity.

5 Stitch these layers together. Remember that a cut edge of Ultrasuede is a finished edge. Nothing will ravel. Edgestitching with a straight stitch is the easiest form of finishing, but you can use satin stitching or decorative stitches. A Teflon foot glides over the Ultrasuede more easily than a basic foot.

Use open, relatively straight decorative stitches on Ultrasuede for embellishment.

6 Don't forget about the keyhole punch for decoration. Use open decorative stitches from the machine. These are the vein stitches from the daisy (color #2) on Floral Dimensions, my embroidery disk.

7 Once the designs are stitched in place, put basting glue on the wrong side of the Ultrasuede in the areas that will be stitched. This includes across the center width for the zipper and the entire outside edge. Work quickly before the glue dries and position the plastic piece to match the edges. If by chance the plastic and Ultrasuede were not cut exactly the same, don't force the edges to meet. Simply match as closely as possible and pat the layers together.

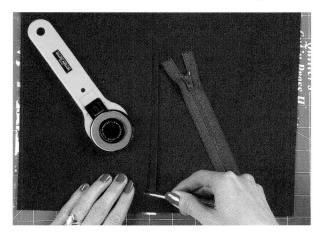

8 Measure the zipper from the top of the slider to the bottom of the stop. Even though you have purchased a 7" zipper, you will be surprised to find this measurement may be 6-7/8" or 7-1/4". To whatever the zipper measures add 1/8" to allow space for the length of the zipper in the opening. Using the rotary cutter, very carefully cut a hole through the Ultrasuede and plastic that is this length by 1/4". There

should be approximately 1" of Ultrasuede at either end of the zipper before the cut edge.

9 Place basting glue on the right side of the zipper tape. Very quickly position the zipper in the hole of the cosmetic case and pat in place. To avoid slippage, allow the glue to dry before stitching. Occasionally the basting glue may dry before it is attached properly. When this happens, hold the iron just above but not touching and give it a shot of steam. This will briefly reactivate the basting glue.

10 Unzip the zipper halfway, fold the Ultrasuede in half with the zipper at the fold and match the corners. Again, do not force any edges to meet as this will cause distortion in the finished bag. Just match the edges as closely as possible. Beginning at the zipper, stitch a 1/4" seam allowance around the outside edge. To avoid making unnecessary holes in the plastic, pin in the seam allowance only.

11 To form the miter at the corners, hold the corner with one hand and place the two seam allowances on top of each other. To hold this position, pin the two stitching lines together. Stitch across the seam allowance to form a triangle. The larger the triangle, the squattier the bag. The smaller the triangle, the taller the bag. I generally plan for this stitching to be approximately 1-1/2" long. It's a choice, but do make each miter the same size.

12 Tie a 1/4" strip of the Ultrasuede you cut for the zipper position to the zipper slider, using a lark's head knot. Even the small pieces never go to waste!

POINT OF INTEREST

✦ Small projects are the perfect opportunity to experiment with new techniques, new tools, or new products.

✦ Before trimming or cutting any shapes from the scraps of Ultrasuede, apply a fusing medium to the wrong side.

✦ Use basting glue to hold layers of Ultrasuede, plastic, and zippers together.

✦ To rejuvenate basting glue once it has dried, hold an iron just above the area and give the glue a shot of steam.

✦ A larger miter results in a boxier bag. A smaller miter makes a taller, narrower bag.

✦ Stitch several decorative lines along the fold of the shoe tote using variegated or decorative thread for a more personal touch.

✦ The lingerie bag and shoe tote may be easily completed on the serger to expedite the process.

Sweater/Lingerie Bag

The lingerie bag is constructed identical to the Inside Hanging Zipper Pocket (page 43). The difference is the size and fabrics used. It is an ideal quick, gift giving project.

Hand washing laundry has never been my idea of fun. I never wash anything by hand that can be thrown in the washing machine. While browsing in the bridal section of a store, I discovered a nylon netting that was strong and durable enough for many washings. I decided it would be perfect to make sweater and lingerie bags. Placing sweaters, pantyhose, and lingerie in the bags before machine washing protects them from damage in the machine.

Later when shopping for more netting, I discovered the store was out of that pattern but I found a netting in the camouflage fabric section that was perfect. The olive green and gray colors weren't so appealing, but luckily I found some white. There were no pretty designs on the netting, but it was strong and ideal for my project.

You will need:

✦ Netting fabric (see *Note*)

✦ Zipper

✦ Thread to match

Note: The amount of netting and the length of the zipper are determined by the size bag you want to make. For pantyhose I use a 12" zipper with netting 13" by approximately 22". The netting is cut 1" wider than the zipper is long by twice the length of the finished bag. There are no hard and fast rules for measurements. Sometimes I work with what I have. To make a lingerie bag use a 14" zipper with the netting 15" by approximately 26". A sweater bag needs an 18" zipper with the netting 19" x 22".

Instructions:

To make the lingerie bag refer to the instructions for the Inside Hanging Zipper Pocket on page 43. The pocket and the bag are made identically. The difference is the size of the zipper and fabric, and the type of fabric. The zipper on the pocket is trimmed to a smaller size while the bag is created the length of the zipper.

These techniques are fun to mix and match with different fabrics for different uses.

SHOE TOTE

While traveling, I have found it handy to have several shoe totes to protect my clothing from my shoes. Rather than a single hole, this tote has two legs so the shoes are kept together yet they don't rub against each other.

You will need:

+ Two 16" or 18" square pieces of fabric (smaller for ladies shoe tote, larger for mens)
+ 12" to 15" of 1/4" elastic
+ Thread to match and for decoration

Instructions:

❶ Lightweight denim or quilting weight cottons are nice fabrics to use for this project because they don't add a lot of bulk in the suitcase. Fold each fabric square in half and place the template on the cut edge and trim around. The fabric will look like a very small pair of pants and the stitching procedure is very similar to sewing a pair of pants.

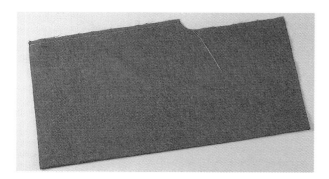

2 Using a 1/4" seam allowance throughout, stitch the straight seam from the template cutout to the other end as shown. Repeat this on the other fabric piece.

3 Turn one leg right side out. Place it inside the other leg, so right sides of each leg face each other. Matching the seam allowance, align the curves from the template cutout and stitch this curved seam, which is like a crotch seam.

4 Pull one leg from inside the other leg and match the seam to the original fold as shown. Stitch across each leg to form the bottom of the tote.

5 At the remaining opening, fold under 1/4", press, and fold an additional 1" to form a casing. Stitch the casing in place, leaving a hole to insert the elastic. Using a safety pin or other tool, pull the elastic through the casing. Experiment with your shoes to determine how tight the elastic should be. I like mine fairly loose since some of my shoes are cumbersome and bulky while others are more streamlined. Stitch the elastic ends together and close the opening.

Shoe tote template

Bags from a Challenge

To stimulate the making of handbags, several years ago I decided to sponsor a challenge on the subject. The rules were very simple. Each entry must include a hardware product from Ghee's (chain, frame, or snap) or a Ghee's pattern. This permitted me to see bags created in the home sewing arena among my students, friends, and whoever chose to enter. It was amazing how many areas of the world participated. Bags arrived in Louisiana from as far away as Australia and Japan. It was like Christmas every day for a while just before the deadline. Actually, the next-day services from the U.S. mail, UPS, and FedEx were still busy on deadline day. For their efforts, there were prizes offered in several categories and each entry received a token gift.

To add inspiration to your sewing, here are a few of the many bags entered in the contest during the several years the contest was held. All names are listed from left to right in the group pictures. All pieces are listed beginning with first place. (*Note:* Many of the entrants have moved since entering the challenge. Their residence is printed as listed on their entry form.)

Sherrie Spangler of Kansas, Joann Ezell of Louisiana, Charleen Pollman of Nebraska, and Nancy Branscom of Arizona.

In her **Flowers in Fuchsia**, first place winner Joann Ezell incorporated 12 machine artistry techniques she learned in her monthly sewing club. Using denim as a base fabric for all, she blended the pieces together with sashing strips of denim stitched randomly with single flowers.

Star Tracks, created by Sherrie Spangler, combined crinkling, couching, double needle, and the cameo shuffle. The braided strap offered diversity to a celestial composition. "This is the first purse I've made in almost 30 years of sewing. It was so much fun that I'm already planning my next one! I'm hooked!"

From embroidery beading to denim, buttons, ribbons, and couching on crinkling, the red, white, and blue color scheme is perfect for **Trial and Tribulation** created by Charlene Pollman. "I received Linda's new book in the mail and was then marooned by flood waters cutting off the highways to town. I used only things I had at home."

Molten Magic, by Nancy Branscom, combined a variety of piecing and thread embellishments. Combinations of cotton and lamé were accented with black. "I wanted to pull all the stops and be as free and creative as possible in design and construction and to use a range of colors I never use."

Sherrie Spangler used **Connected** to display a mirage of crinkled fabric with tassels, couching, free-motion quilting, thread lace from Sharee Dawn Roberts, and bias tubes to connect the techniques. "I challenged myself to keep the design simple, but every time I tried to stop I got the urge to embellish just one more area!"

Florence Johnson created a triple cameo to show several inserts on **Are There Black Holes In Space?** Using only fabrics in black and the right and wrong side of the denim added interesting contrast. "Curved prairie points are much more pleasing to my eye than the more common method of them meeting at corners on quilts."

Was **Fish** inspired by an almost all night sewing class one snowy night in Maryland? "These fish purses have been very popular. There is something humorous and offbeat about them that people find appealing. I make them in several sizes and with all sorts of fabrics and embellishments," says Sandra Sapienza.

Florence Johnson of Alberta, Canada, Sherrie Spangler of Texas, and Sandra Sapienza of Maryland.

Sylvia Polk of California, Linda Koch of Florida, and Janet Ike of Oregon.

A certified scuba diver, Linda Koch saw five large sea turtles on her first turtle watch expedition. This inspired **Friends Beneath the Sea** as her entry of crinkling, couching, reverse appliqué, puffed appliqué, drippling, melange, free-motion embroidery, and piece quilting. The matching coat placed in the Sulky Challenge the same year.

Using a basically black background of a collage of fabrics, Sylvia Polk free-motion embroidered flowers with brilliant shades of Luny yarn and rayon and metallic threads to create **Night Flower**. Clusters of machine sewn seed beads added a realistic finish to the centers.

Janet Ike enjoys searching for old beautiful embellishments for her work. The antique Czechoslovakian crystal buckle for the closure and old house key make a perfect finish for silk charmeuse and old lace crinkled, lattice piecing with decorative stitching. "I challenged myself to create something old with new methods and technology for **Silk 'n Lace**."

Linda Johnston combined the glitter of lamé and metallic trims with the darkness of black velvet to construct a silhouette of the city. "I love black with a little red and silver for special evenings out. I decided to make this bag for nights when I was really going to **Paint the Town Red**. The skyline of the city is turning red as the partying heats up."

After spritzing her fabric with tumble dyes, Janice Zenor hopped into an Easter theme. She selected bright buttons rather than pins to create a variation of bobbin lace using twisted, textured yarns for **A Tisket A Tasket, I Put All My Eggs In One Basket**. The dyed band with the large button at the top pulls the bag together for a practical finish.

Albert, the eight-year-old grandson of Barbara Null, drew a picture of an elephant in school as part of an art show in a local bank. They collaborated in collecting materials for three months to make **Albert's Elephant**. Crink-

The Judges' Choice awards went to Janet Ike of Oregon, Linda Johnston of New Jersey, Janice Zenor of California, and Barbara Null of Pennsylvania.

First place for the 1996 awards went to Janet Ike of Oregon.

ling, couching, puffing, and chenille add texture. No elephant handbag is complete without an insect button by his ear.

"Linda's books have totally changed my sewing projects from mundane to creative gallery art!" Inspired by the fruit on the vine while touring the Alderbrook Winery in Healdsburg, California, Janet Ike combined lattice piecing, crinkling, thread embellishment and 3-D embroidery with cotton, sheers, and lamé to complete **Harvest '96**.

Inspired by the old song of a similar name, Anne Sheikh designed **A Tisket A Tasket, A Purple and Yellow Basket** totally of white silk douppioni. The realistic fabric basket is filled with dyed 3-D flowers, accented with rhinestones and Kreinik thread and wrapped in a bow. On the corded handles by the opening appears a butterfly. The piece is so real it doesn't look like a handbag.

For Stephanie Kimura, the silk, lace, and pearl mode evolved after working with a client and seven bridesmaid dresses. "**Hearts Desire** made me think about youth, truth, idealism, and love." Composed of cut edge 3-D appliqué, free-motion embroidery, thread embellishment with pearls and beads on silk, laces, and lamé.

Anne Sheikh of California.

Stephanie Kimura of Florida.

For her first beading project, Leslie Holder created **If Judith Leiber Rode a Hog** entirely of handwork. Accented with the Harley-Davidson insignia and Kreinik threads, the strap is actually a timing chain. "I've always admired Judith Leiber's work, especially the exquisite minaudières she does so well. Ghee's Challenge provided the opportunity for me to pay homage."

Tied with herself for second place, Stephanie Kimura was inspired by a dive trip to the Bahamas. Shades of purple, blue, and turquoise silk were gathered and crinkled to form the illusion of water. Metallic threads for glitter were free-motion stitched and arranged into tassels for the texture of plant life in **Come "Sea" Us In Florida**.

Leslie Holder of Louisiana.

Stephanie Kimura of Florida.

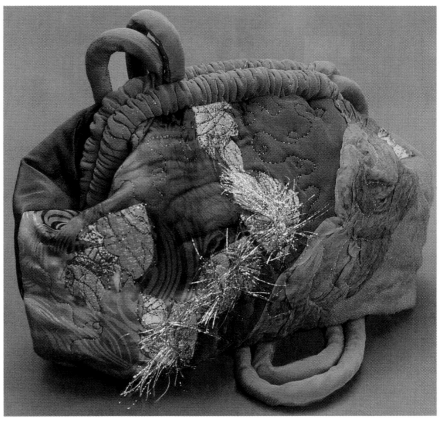

Jayne Butler, a fiber artist formerly from Australia, incorporated her love of fabric sculpture — the manipulating of traditional fabrics, threads, yarns, and metals into extraordinary works of art — in **A Touch of Class**, shown at right in the photo. The lace trim along the edge was created solely from decorative threads machine stitched on a wash-away base, leaving only thread loops chained together.

Jayne Butler of California.

Stephanie Kimura's desire to **See America** led her to create a backpack and a big one at that, to travel the states and venture into every fabric store in America. Beginning her journey at the Houston Quilt Festival, she carried her tote of recycled blue jeans combined with Ultrasuede and metallic threads using 3-D appliqué and buttons for accent.

Stephanie Kimura of Florida.

Part of an ensemble of two outfits that won first place for "Spectacular Adornment" at the Bazaar Del Mundo Fashion Show, Anne Sheikh added to her collection of spectacular 3-D floral baskets. The shimmer of beads, sequins, and rhinestones suggest realism for **Aunt Fiona's Funky Flower Patch**. No flower garden is ever complete without the occasional fly!

Anne Sheikh of California.

No flower is ever complete without the occasional fly!

Fancy Bags with Leftovers

It's my passion to experiment with as many types of sewing and needle arts as any one person could. Whether working with fabric and threads to add texture, free-motion embroidery, machine embroidery, strip piecing, making blocks, heirloom sewing, or appliqué, I'm always willing to venture into something new.

Many times I quickly find out that the thing I try isn't something I want to pursue. Other times I discover that I prefer to continue the project using different colors of thread or fabric. Whatever the experiment, it is never in vain, because I learn something. Whether I like it or not, I still learn something.

In the trial run, the test piece is always large enough to make a bag or a portion of one. Maybe I build the piece larger with combinations of other experiments or leftovers. Perhaps the small piece becomes the pocket. These test samplers are the reason I have so many examples to show in my classes — several hundred I believe, although I have never really counted!

On the other hand, when I discover a technique I enjoy, I make lots of it. I would rather have leftover pieces than run short, so I make more. The original plan begins with a garment. After the garment is made, the leftovers go into a bag to complete the ensemble. That's the plan.

Many times when I begin to make a garment I haven't a clue which pattern I'm going to use. I may have an idea, but I always leave my mind open for new brainstorms that arise as my project is in motion.

Other things are important to me too. Because I live in Louisiana and have no great need for coats, I have a tendency to make vests. The vest is the third piece in an ensemble (the blouse and skirt or pants are one and two) that completes the look or ties the wardrobe together. If the truth really be told, I'm not fond of setting in sleeves, making lapels, or fitting. A vest suits me just fine.

Consider some of these ideas when making your next garment. Include techniques you enjoy doing on garments that are fun to make. It's nice to make a fashion statement and carry the handbag you would never leave home without.

Every wardrobe's basic necessity — comfortable and casual with the allure of simplicity for easygoing gadding about — requires that third piece. To complete the well-rounded wardrobe, choose a handbag to match! This sporty vest to wear anywhere and over so many things is composed with a sampler of machine techniques. Each separate unit is constructed larger than necessary. Once I finished the vest, I chose the style for the handbag based on the leftovers.

Crinkled and couched fabric forms the uppermost section of this hobo-shaped bag. The spiral patchwork and flying geese separate it from the two types of pintucking created at the bottom of the bag. Gold purchased corded piping divides the front piece from the back. If the design on the front doesn't match the design on the back it is less noticeable with the corded piping. A chain is appropriate for this size bag, but a larger bag would require a fabric strap. This use of leftovers makes a contrasting bag yet offers the perfect companion for the outfit.

The sophisticated traveler travels in style with a tapestry vest and bag to match. Don't overlook tapestry for work or pleasure. When choosing tapestry for a bag, consider the weight. While most tapestries are perfect for the body of a bag, many are too heavy to use for the strap and piping. Contrasting fabrics and colors are

better for these areas. Ultrasuede makes a very durable fabric for the straps and opening area of the bag, and adds the contrast in the piping, necessary for design. They are perfectly compatible to make a coordinated statement.

A reminder in cutting the tapestry: be sure the design is centered high on the bag. Many handbag patterns include a bottom seam. The actual visible section of the bag is much higher since some of the fabric forms the bottom of the bag. Choose a section of the tapestry that best suits this area of the bag. It should generally be different than the predominate design shown on the garment. Be certain you understand the style bag you are creating to avoid disappointment later. This is a most versatile bag to sling over the shoulder and go anywhere. It's so versatile you'll wear it over and over again with everything.

An excellent companion for a prolonged season of wear is a lattice pieced vest. Wear it with lighter colors for the spring and fall, then add darker shades for the winter months. The base garment pulls out different strips of fabric in the piecing, changing the overall color scheme.

The lattice piecing begins with a large piece of fabric and continues by cutting and inserting strips to pull the fabric back together again. Described in detail in my book *Creating Texture With Textiles*, lattice piecing is a very simple and relatively quick piecing method. Designed and created by my aunt, Toto McGehee, **Purple Heather**, is the perfect vest for the lady who loves to wear purple.

A perfectly coordinated vest and bag require far too much matching when working with the lattice piecing. It's too much of a good thing. A slight contrast is necessary for the bag to show up in the outfit. Another time a pieced bag would be perfect with a solid outfit. Determine when you plan to use the bag.

For a new approach, free-motion embroidery is added to the center panel. The detachable pin designed and created by Jayne Butler is the focal point of this area. The purple background of the pin blended far too much with the piecing, hiding the free-motion thistle stitched with yarn and metallic thread. The needle lace edging disappeared. By changing the center panel of the bag to the crinkled violet fabric and stitching with the same variegated metallic as the pin, each section has its own definition and nothing is hidden. To tie

the lattice piecing side panels with the center panel requires framework. Double corded piping with large purple and smaller jade corded piping finishes the bag. It brings everything together, yet gives definition to each segment of the bag. Gold double link chain may be dropped into the bag when a clutch is preferred.

Radiant, with the brilliancy of harmonious color, this classic pair adds to easy dressing. Every wardrobe's basic necessity to ease over a simple dress, skirts, trousers, or jeans includes piecework.

The spiral patchwork begins with rows of strip piecing. To insure there are enough fabric strips to make the garment, several sections are sewn together as described in *Creating Texture With Textiles*. The difference from this piecing and the instructions in the book is that this project is made on the serger with the three-thread narrow rolled hem, using woolly nylon metallic in the upper looper and basic thread in the lower looper and needle. The strips are stitched wrong sides together so the narrow rolled edge shows, giving

the illusion that a tiny corded piping is included between each seam allowance. After referring to the chapter on Spiral Piecing in *Creating Texture With Textiles*, follow the process using the serger, except serge the strips with the right side out or wrong sides together. This is backwards from the normal procedure.

Believe it or not, the serger patchwork is much faster than the straight stitch machine, since all the design is accomplished in one stitching and the ironing is minimal. A narrow strip of corded piping repeating the three-thread rolled hem is inserted in the vertical seams of the piecing. This is just enough contrast to distinguish between the strips and add character to the garment. Note the undisciplined striped fabric is cut on the lengthwise as well as the crosswise grain for variety. I enjoy cutting stripes and plaids in this manner to add diversity using the same fabric.

To assemble the handbag, I chose a pouchy, gathered design. The ripples force the straight lines in the piecing to become tucked and pleated. The straight lines are distorted, offering variety to a nicely proportioned bag necessary for this perfectly coordinated wardrobe basic.

Stroll through the day and on into the evening with another pieced garment. The blend of purples combined with the subtle hint of embroidery and metallic lace trim offers perfect simplicity for complicated days.

Linda's Vest pattern (Ghee's, see Resources) includes instructions to make the fan design. Two sets of strips, each approximately 16" wide, are sewn together. Shapes are cut from the strips, using the seams as the grain line, with the Starmaker 5 tool by Kaye Wood. An 18° wedge offers the perfect slant to build the piecing back together. Probably the quickest piecing idea I have tried, 45" strips are ample to make the vest and have plenty leftover for a bag.

To add variety to the bag, the fan design is centered in the middle section with a combination of the remaining fabrics from the piecing used to fill in the sides. Gold corded piping separates and defines each section, yet pulls the bag together. Since gold cluny lace was introduced between the piecing, the gold corded piping fits nicely into the bag. A chain or small strap is appropriate to use as the handle for an outfit that is truly uncomplicated, yet has a simple elegance with a creative perspective.

A fresh mix of texture and color makes an ingenious answer to easy evening dressing. The crinkled white-on-white fabric is dyed using Tumble Dye. It is quick and easy to use these spray-on dyes and no great artistic ability is necessary. The dyeing chapter in *Creating Texture With Textiles* demonstrates several folding and wadding techniques to add personality to a white fabric. Once the fabric is dyed and set, rows and rows of heavier yarns, twisted Candlelight, and metallic edge 1/8" ribbon are couched into place to totally change the appearance of the crinkled, dyed, white-on-white fabric.

A small bag lends itself to evening wear. This one is toned down quite a bit from the vest, making the vest the most prominent part of the outfit. Only the metallic edged ribbon is couched into place for decoration. A double layer of variegated Ultrasheen, a shiny, bright thread, is passed through one needle. The overlapping colors blend and change frequently as the entredeux stitch meanders with the ribbon. Unplanned or programmed stitching can be very relaxing and creative with very little effort.

Worn over a soft flowing dress or tapered-leg pant, a highly embellished vest/bag ensemble creates quite a stir at evening or holiday events.

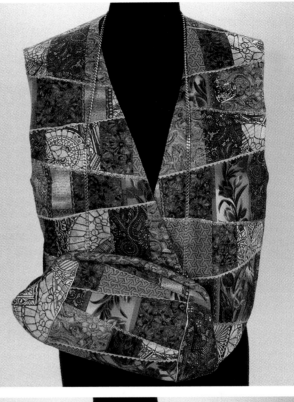

Dressing beautifully just got a lot simpler with an elongated slightly fitted vest, so comfortable and casual yet lovely to harmonize for special occasions. A permanent corsage features embroidery from Floral Dimensions, a disk digitized by Cactus Punch to create very realistic flowers. I wanted the flowers from my garden to last longer and my embroidery disk allows me to surround myself with wonderful flowers that last forever and don't have to be watered or cared for.

The base of the garment is constructed from spiral patchwork with couching of Candlelight. The added sparkle from the thread ties in with the Reflections thread used in the flowers. Larger corded piping accents the shoulder area of the garment, pulling the eye towards the flowers and face.

After evaluating the size and shape of the leftover strips, I realized that a rectangular shaped bag was the answer. Though many designs from ready-to-wear are narrow and elongated, this bag is 9" wide because that was the width of the leftover fabric. The shortest of the strips was long enough to make the bag 11" deep. Not a planned shape, but one that works with a longer vest. The oversize brown corded piping and a bouquet of smaller flowers add elegance to an utterly comfortable welcome wardrobe addition.

⊹ *Never let a scrap of fabric go to waste. Make a handbag.*

⊹ *Determine the size and style bag by the shapes and amount of left-overs.*

⊹ *Center the focal point high on the bag to avoid having the predominate design fall to the bottom.*

⊹ *Introduce another form of embellishment on the bag to avoid too much of one technique.*

⊹ *Choose a contrasting shape of bag from the design in the garment. A vest with many straight lines complements a pouchy bag.*

⊹ *To add variety to a pieced bag, fill in the side panels with larger pieces of remaining fabrics.*

⊹ *Use more decoration either on the bag or on the garment to add variety.*

Creative Bags From Designers

Handbags, whether for day or evening, may be practical or whimsical. They may be useful or arty; for everyday or for a special event. All handbags should be fun. Your attitude may be revealed and displayed by the handbag you carry. Here are some ideas from designers and friends who have used handbags to showcase their unique talents.

This is the conversation overheard before class one day in Florida. "Who would ever carry that?" came the first remark. "Oh, I would, just for fun," came the response from her friend. "I'm going to make one for my granddaughter. She loves fish and she can use it as a pajama bag on her bed until she grows up and can carry it. She's only five," a third friend added. "Hey, that's not a bad idea, I'll have to rethink this," was the response from the first. Then it was time for class to begin. Sometimes it doesn't matter if the project is practical. Do it for fun, just like Sandra Sapienza from Maryland did.

Sandra Sapienza.

On the other hand, practical can be fun too. Picking a handbag this season is a snap, thanks to Jeanine Twigg of The Snap Source in Michigan. She textured fleece fabric using a computer embroidery design disk for the base of the purse. The flap, made with a complementary woven fabric, uses fashion colored snaps for security and decoration. The detachable strap uses two sets of snaps on each end for added strength to hold the weight of the bag and easy removal when a clutch is desired. Inside, a key ring and small change purse snap securely to the lining to avoid losing the little but important things that tend to fall to the bottom of the bag. These are clever ideas to stay organized and avoid frustration. One word of advice from Jeanine is to stitch with fleece next to the feed dogs and woven fashion fabric next to the pressure foot when possible.

Jeanine Twigg.

Michele Hester of Missouri used Fiber-Etch fabric remover to complete her striking bag (the top bag in the photo below). Just apply, iron, and rinse to make cutwork, appliqué, embroidery and so much more. Fibers are removed cleanly and easily from fabrics originating from plant matter. This includes cotton, linen, rayon, and paper. For variety, select a fabric blend like silk/linen or wool/rayon. Fiber-Etch will remove only the plant fibers, etching a design in the remaining fibers. Stitch with silk or 100% synthetic thread like Ultrasheen acrylic. Michele also uses paints and sand art as an edging for decorative enhance-ments and texture for timesaving cutwork with-out tedious cutting.

Free-motion beadwork, machine stitched on suede by Theta Happ of Oklahoma gives an evening bag a special glitter for the night on the town (the bottom bag in the photo below). I've had the opportunity to teach at Theta's on several occasions. One evening she took the last tid-bits of a piece of fringed beading and cross-locked beads to create this gorgeous bag. It's amazing how a few leftovers can be combined to create something wonderful. Many times the left-overs determine what the design will be.

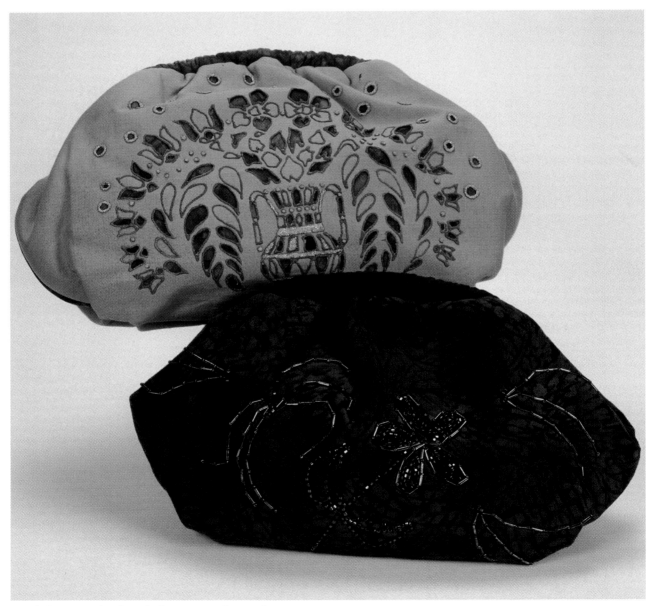

Michele Hester (top) and Theta Happ (bottom).

Verna Holt.

Verna Holt created the most wonderful free-motion machine work. She can use the machine needle like it was a paintbrush. Combining rayon and metallic thread, the magnolia embroidery is as realistic as the blooms outside my window in the summer.

A professional fabric designer and quilt maker, Marty Lawrence of Kwilts & Kloze in Michigan hand dyes fabrics to create surface design. She uses shades of a color for gradations. Streaked colors are created by twisting or knotting lengths of fabric. Using only hand dyes in a project or combinations of hand dyes and printed fabric combine to make wonderful quilted projects. The usage of the right side of the fabric and the other side of the fabric adds a subtle contrast in piecing for a shoulder bag or a clutch.

Marty Lawrence.

Combining wearable art and serging, Diane Bossom of Texas has used her artistic talents to put the seams on the outside rather than the inside. Among the many ideas in her book *Serge Art,* she made an Ultra Crazy Vest using the Ultrasuede scraps from her collection. Of course she needed a bag to match. She set the serger for a two- or three-thread flat-lock stitch using decorative thread in the needle and polyester serger thread in the other positions. Then she set the stitch width and length between 1 and 2 and serged all the patchwork together before cutting the panel for the bag. It is so easy to create contemporary artwork on the serger.

The beautiful textured look of created cotton chenille is featured in these three **Innovative** purses designed by the ladies at Four Corners Designs, Inc. in Texas. The technique, revived from years ago, is really quite simple. To make chenille, stack several layers of fabric together and stitch through all the layers to form quilting lines. Slash through all the layers except the bottom layer, which forms the base. Wash the fabric to cause the layers to "blossom" like traditional chenille.

It is presented in several shapes including rectangular using the magnetic snap on the flap for closure. The other two

curved shapes use a button loop to hold the opening secure. Adapt Shadow Chenille or chenille appliqué to any pattern to add variety and dimension.

Diane Bossom.

Four Corners Designs, Inc.

Judee Bequette of Oklahoma is a tolé painter and fabric painter who loves working with silk. Several years ago she designed a silk ensemble for the prestigious Fairfield Style Show. Completing her outfit was this gorgeous vibrant yellow Ultrasuede handbag with detailed floral painting.

Judee Bequette.

Silk ribbon and crazy quilt designer and teacher, Betty Caskey of Alberta, Canada, uses bias cut ribbon, wire edge ribbon, and silk ribbon to detail her smart **Bridal Bag** and **Opera Purse**. A connoisseur of fine handwork with decorative threads and beads, Betty incorporates lace with several shades of white to cream for the delicate bridal bag. A small magnetic snap inserted in the flap offers a secure closing. The button trimmed with lace and a tassel add a complimentary finish of fine detail. Crazy quilting using several shades of black ribbon, silk, brocade, decorative threads and buttons, complete with a twisted cord for piping and strap, make the small bag proper for any evening or black tie affair.

Betty Caskey.

Capture a view with textiles. Linda Crone of Illinois has the ability to combine a variety of printed or solid fabrics with decorative threads to duplicate a special scene from nature or create an imaginative one. Her book, *Fabric Landscapes by Machine*, shows her simplified techniques of manipulating fabrics, combining textures, and blending thread to transform fabric into art. **Plentiful Pockets** offers the palette for a small scene in the purse, and a larger landscape on the tote. Use appropriate straps for each size. A small magnetic snap on the smaller version and one or two large magnetic snaps on the large bag offer the same closure as designer bags.

Linda Crone.

The **Zipped Up Tote** is a versatile, roomy tote that when unzipped becomes a handy 36" square flat surface, adaptable to many occasions. It works well as a picnic tote, complete with table-cloth. The silverware and plates fit in the side pocket. Lunch or wine and cheese are carried in the tote to the table or grassy spot. The swimming tote opens to a beach towel. The baby tote becomes a changing pad. The choice of fabrics is determined by the end use. The bag can be embellished to suit the recipient or occasion. The pocket size is adjustable to accommodate a specific item or can be omitted entirely. Designed by Anne Carr of Arizona, this unique idea for a tote is truly a quick, easy idea for gift giving at weddings or baby showers.

Linda Nakashima of Illinois is known for her exquisite Russian punch needle embroidery. She uses other needles to accommodate other weaves of fabric or sizes of thread. She uses woven fabric as a base for the needle punch with short thread loops, long thread loops, and fringe. Raw silk or Ultrasuede create a mat to show the impeccable detail. Every stitch is in place. Various decorative threads from cotton to metallic decorate Linda's designs. To add a

Anne Carr.

contrasting texture, many times a shell is inserted into the thread work. Elegance with style is the way to describe her work.

Linda Nakashima.

The **Silk Moth Bag** created by Donna Rhodes of Florida, uses a base of fulled wool and hand-made silk/camel-down felt foundation for the embroidery and beadwork. To make the fulled wool, Donna washed the fabric several times and dried it extra long in the dryer to make the fibers mat together much like boiled wool. In the actual felting process, in this case the moth body that is made of silk and camel down, the wool is combed or carded into a web or batt. The batts are layered at 90 degree angles to each other and sewn between two pieces of muslin. Washing this bundle causes the fabric to felt or mat together.

Once they are thoroughly matted and start shrinking into a compact mass, the process is called fulling.

An advocate of handwork, Donna freehand stylized the silk moth design using embroidery with silk, metallic, and cotton floss; beads and sequins; hand-dyed silk ribbon, Sulky thread lace, and embroidery leftovers. The techniques include padded satin stitch, chain stitch, feather stitch, stem stitch, whipped running stitch, looped stitch, French knots, straight stitch, composite stitches, and beading. The wrapped wire techniques used in the moth body are described in *Warped Women and Material Men*, a book by Warp and Woof Creations. Using the same shape as the front but different artistic treatment, the back incorporates twin-needle stitching, couching, lace making, and free-hand thread sketching completed on the machine. To add more texture to the bag, Donna finished with vintage buttons, feathers, and a gar fish scale. There's just no end to the possibilities of combinations a designer will use.

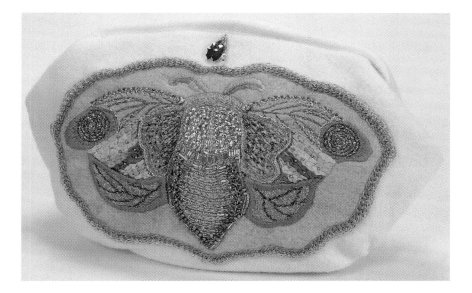

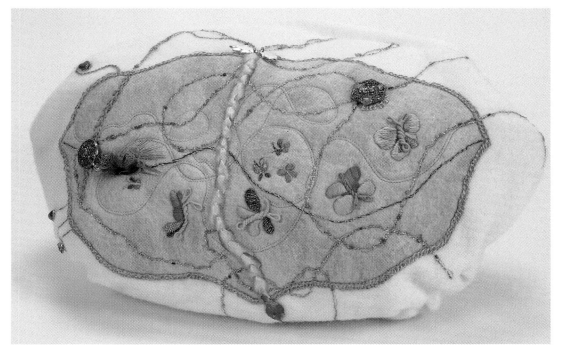

Donna Rhodes.

Not a suitcase, this **Sling Bag/Purse** conveniently carries a cellular phone, appointment diary, checkbook, sunglasses, and all the smaller necessities of life. It also provides a blank slate for creative embellishment. On her bag, Connie Hester of Texas features foundation piecing from her book, *Improvisational Design in Quilts Using Paper Foundations*. The other bag includes embellishment of assorted buttons, although a collection of small found objects could be used instead. Both bags use heavier corded piping for detail and a large magnetic snap as the closure. Leave it to Connie to come up with the ingenious idea of using purchased belts as straps!

Connie Hester.

Fabulous Cutwork in Ultrasuede by Ann Wall of Texas offers a new look at conventional cutwork by incorporating Ultrasuede, a fabric that doesn't ravel. Ann uses a double layer in the process, cutting the upper layer with very sharp pointed scissors and positioning it on the second layer. Instead of the traditional zigzag, she chose straight stitching, which makes it easier to stitch next to the edge. A quicker, very 90s update to a very traditional method.

Ann Wall.

Double Deep Cloth, a creation of Kathy Stachowicz from Florida, follows techniques from *The Fine Art of Pin-weaving, Creative Variations*. The basic idea of the weaving used in pot holders takes on a very new meaning when Kathy uses hand-dyed yarns, boucle, thick and thin yarn, and nubby yarn. She employed Toob yarn manipulation from the book *Darn Good Yarn Tricks*, plain weave, Soumak, chaining, slits (both diagonal and interlocking), beaded warp, and knotting. Toob is a knitted yarn in the round, resulting in a tubular yarn. With Kathy's technique, a needle is pushed through the tube to gather the yarn for more texture. Soumak is a handweaving stitch incorporated into pin weaving to add dimension.

To vary the texture, Kathy wove handmade clay and glass beads with fabric strips, novelty yarns, and applied ribbon embellishment with Artemis Silk Ribbon. This is weaving with an attitude — the desire to get attention.

Kathy Stachowicz.

Needlework of all types merges into handbags easily with Ultrasuede or other fabrics used to fill in the spaces. Linda Ferguson of Louisiana created **All That Glitters** using embroidery on canvas, a technique she learned in a class under Marnie Ritter at Callaway Gardens School of Needlearts. All the threads are metallic. Some of the sampler of the stitches are done traditionally, while others are on the bias. A double corded piping frames the handwork. The other selection, a Barzello panel, is inserted between crinkled and couched linen. I recall the day someone said they were so happy to have a place to put their handwork other than on a pillow or a wall.

Linda Ferguson.

The **Triangulation** purse was created one morning during breakfast. Michelle Wilman of Calgary, Alberta, quickly took the cereal box and started to cut and fold. In her excitement, she ran to her sewing machine and began pulling fabrics and threads in her favorite colors. There's nothing like pink and orange to get the blood flowing! She chose some favorite buttons from her collection and charms that delight; yarns, ribbons, and beads for the cording, and viola! This purse was truly a vision turned reality. The fun was in the process. Now it's a pattern for all to enjoy and make.

Michelle Wilman.

Who would ever expect denim to turn into this wonderful scene of a gigantic oak overlooking a bay from a mountainous cliff? Bambi Stadler of California has a way of combining free-motion embroidery and appliqué with bobbin work and cutwork to make the most realistic pictures. **Fabric Pizza** combines itsy bitsy pieces of thread, fabric, souvenirs, latex balloons, gift wrapping, yarn, and other things lying around the sewing room floor and places them between a fabric base and plastic. The layers are randomly stitched together. Ultrasuede makes a suitable contrast for corded piping and casing. These are eye-catching works of art suitable for display or to carry the necessities of the day.

Bambi Stadler.

Fabric manipulation and free-motion embroidery are the focus of much of Jayne Butler's work. Originally from Australia and currently a resident of California, Jayne has a manner of combining traditional yarns and threads into not-so-traditional formations. Her use of needle lace — a technique where decorative threads in the needle and bobbin are stitched on a wash-away stabilizer to create lace edging along the flap of the bag — completes the decorative work from the flap. Stipple quilting with metallic threads holds the layers of backing and fabric. A magnetic snap secures the flap in place. Yarn is woven through the chain for a Chanel look that adds the finishing touch to remarkable bags.

Jayne Butler.

Kuba cloth is native to the Shoowa people of the kingdom of Kuba that lies today in the Democratic Republic of Congo in Central Africa. Kuba velvet as shown in this **Picnic Tote** by Ronke Luke-Boone is amazing on many levels. It is made from natural fiber-grass and raffia. It is characterized by the geometric rectilinear designs such as shown on this piece. The complex designs are free-flowing. They are made without prior planning using unknotted, very tightly woven tufts of raffia threaded between the weft and the warp and cut very close to the fabric surface. Kuba cloth comes in rich earth colors of natural, rich red, ochre, and black. Kuba cloth has been used in garments, shrouds, and even as a type of currency. Formerly from Africa and now a resident of Virginia, Ronke designed her tote pattern using Kuba cloth with leather. Two large magnetic snaps secure the bag at the upper edge where the double straps are attached and feet protect the bottom from wear.

Ronke Luke-Boone

Explore, expand, and express **Creative Options** with Annrae Roberts of New Mexico. Her lighthearted approach to stitching allows freedom to stretch and develop each project with the creative juices flowing. A firm believer that there is more than one way of doing, saying, being, and thinking about everything, Annrae proposes there's more than one right answer. Beginning with Annrae's Wonder Weave technique, these bags use tubes of a variety of fabrics in graded or contrasting color waves as the base for decorative stitching and embellishment. Free-motion embroidery, shag, tassels, and other collage effects with cloth techniques decorate the flaps, which are secured with a magnetic snap. Decorative cord and braided fabric strips with tassels form the straps to finish the bags. Cultivate visions, plant some seeds to get started, add a few tips and tricks for fertilizer, and top it off with a colorful rainbow.

Annrae Roberts.

Virginia Avery.

Shirley Botsford.

It's a Bag! It's a Tote! It's Terrific! by Virginia Avery of New York, showcases her love of wearable art. A frequent contributor to the prestigious Fairfield Fashion Show, Virginia believes the wearable art movement of today is still closely woven into the quilt world, even though not all artists are quilters. Her light-hearted approach to stitching, using scraps to design and stitch directly to foundation, makes her projects fun, fast, and attention getters on the sidewalk or runway. She uses a collage method called Avery's fabricage, stitch and flip, or quilt and embellish to decorate the surface of the bag or tote. The gusset for the tote forms the shoulder strap. Bias binding encases the seams to finish the edges. This multi-sized bag can be made any size you want. Just remember — don't make it any larger than you are willing to carry it full!

Shirley Botsford's award-winning purse design received the American Quilter's Society "Best Of Show" award. Perfect as an evening bag, bride's bag, or showcase for your own special fabric collection, this easy-to-stitch project can be made in two versatile sizes. Choose casual fabrics, gathered strips of fancy fabrics, or *Daddy's Ties* to create **A Pouf of a Purse**. Customize the quilted flap with decorative stitching and other collectibles. Hold it secure with the magnetic snap. The braided strap of fabrics is just the right finishing touch. Shirley's been involved in every aspect of sewing and needle arts. Her studio, Botsford Briar, is an 1889 Queen Anne Victorian home in New York's Hudson River Valley, where she works and holds retreats for quilters and stitchers.

Known for her reversible garments and quilts, Anita Murphy of Texas, surprised me with the **Magic Bag**. It comes home with you from the grocery store along with all the other bags and holds only one ingredient — sugar. With very little care and effort, a piece of ribbon or yarn transforms the empty sugar bag into a **Candy Bag**. Anita travels with this sturdy paper bag to quilt classes, schools, lectures, and tours. She is known to travel with her Candy Bag and many will bring bags of candy to add to the bag as it needs refills. Truly, some of the Magic comes from sharing, caring, and bringing a smile. Often this small treat makes dear and lasting friendships.

To make the bag, open the top of the sugar bag very carefully so as not to tear the sealed edges. After removing all the sugar, fold down approximately 3" of the top to the inside of the bag. This is usually where the printing begins. Make a firm crease at the top. Use a sturdy hole punch to make two holes on the front and two holes on the back about 1" in from the sides. Insert ribbon or yarn from the outside to the inside to form the handles. Knot the ribbon large enough so it won't slip out and fill with your favorite individually wrapped candy. Anita is quick to add that there is usually a bonus on every bag, a free recipe. I never dreamed I would shop for sugar for the packaging rather than the brand or price. Every sugar company has its own unique constantly changing packaging. Now let's go to the fancy cookie section and try our luck with foil bags!

An artist, designer, and teacher, Carole Liebzeit of Ohio has traveled the globe, collecting fabrics, trims, and trinkets along the way. Each of these bags accompanied a Fairfield garment made by Carole. Her unusual use of stripes accents the patchwork and strip piecing. I was curious to see the black and white piecing in 1" blocks matching so perfectly, only to

discover that it was a printed fabric. What luck to find such a piece! Decorated with buttons for the finishing touches, these bags are the perfect accessory for the coats they were designed for.

Anita Murphy.

Carole Liebzeit.

Many of the techniques traditionally completed by hand are now easily accomplished on the sewing machine. Betty Farrell and Marie Duncan of Illinois are two machine-aholics who have discovered the ease of making ribbon embroidery quicker and easier by machine. It takes a fine eye to know whether some of their work is by hand or machine. Together, they have several books on handwork by machine, but this dainty handbag graced the cover of *More Ribbon Embroidery by Machine*. A collector and frequent visitor to antique stores, Betty discovered this wonderful frame, the perfect closure to an elegant bag.

Betty Farrell and Marie Duncan.

Now it is possible to do foundation quilt block piecing on pre-printed fabric. New and accomplished quilters are excited to sew quilt blocks without having to cut templates and fabric shapes before they begin piecing. Sharon Hultgren of Minnesota has designed **Foundation by the Yard** for machine or hand piecing. Stitch the number of blocks necessary for the bag size. There is no paper to tear away when the blocks are finished. The fabric backing becomes the added layer for stabilizing. The clutch uses piecing on one side of the bag with a complementary fabric on the other. The fold-over allows the piecing to show on both sides. Use corded piping to accent the edge, a cluster of buttons for decoration, and the magnetic snap for closing. This is the perfect quick project to experiment with a new technique and color combinations.

Sharon Hultgren.

These bags are among the ones submitted for a designer showcase. They are listed clockwise from left to right. Carole Nicholas of Virginia, Chungie Lee of Seoul, Korea, Judy Bishop of California, Jenny Raymond of Nebraska, Beth Schwartz Wheeler of Virginia, Susan Deal of Arizona, Ann Wall of Texas, and Sharon Commins of California.

Carole Nicholas' novelty handbag (first from left, back row) was created to wear with a vest using tulle over cutout shapes. It reminds Carole of her island home of Jamaica, particularly the undersea world, with its fantastic colors and creatures.

Chungie Lee is intrigued by the freeform 3-D space potential (second bag from left, back row). "I think my work is a rough draft of design. My design concept is recycling," says Chungie. She used the back side of a high school military training top as the ground fabric of the bag, and incorporated the remaining partial part as pockets on the surface of the bag. The actual pockets from the uniform add an additional layer of pockets for organization. Chungie serged red thread to add color variety to this practical tote.

The inspiration for the handbag by Judy Bishop (third from left, back row) came from a multi-stripe fabric by John Kaldor. The plain beige fabric was first embellished using textured surface techniques of twin needle, couching, and doodling. The fabric was cut into irregular shapes and bound with striped fabric to form **Textured Treasures**. Geometric shapes were cut from the solid fabrics, frayed and appliquéd and quilted onto the main fabric. Additional beading adds detail to the flap, which closes with a magnetic snap.

Influenced by a Threadplay class with Libby Lehman, Jenny Raymond incorporated her new knowledge with double needle, couching, and quilting to make a hobo style bag (fourth from left, back row). The large surface offered the opportunity for combinations of techniques. The geometric design of purples and turquoise was accented with shades of gold.

Carole Nicholas, Chungie Lee, Judy Bishop, Jenny Raymond, Beth Schwartz Wheeler, Susan Deal, Ann Wall, Sharon Commins.

Made with scraps from her Fairfield garment, Beth Schwartz Wheeler created her own envelope style bag with a flap and magnetic snap closure (fourth from left, front row). The postcard images were painted on fabric using Marjorie Croner's patented process described in her book, *Fabric Photos*. Yards and yards of gold metallic threadwork were added to enhance the piecing and large cording finished the edges. A decorative button and tassel offered the appropriate trim and finishing touches.

Having a couple of great pig fabrics and lots of silk in her collection, Susan Deal decided that, **Yes, You Can Make A Silk Purse Out of a Sow's Ear** (third from left, front row). The pieced design on the bag is a traditional quilt block often known as "monkey wrench." (All blocks have alternate names. The other name for this block is "pig's tail.") Susan embellished the intersection of the blocks with some silver pig charms. The lining is another pig print that shows a store window with a sow's ear purse for sale.

Silver Fantasy by Ann Wall (second from left, front row) displays her unusual cutwork designs. Silver lamé as the base fabric shadows through the Ultrasuede with ultimate detail. The contrast in texture and color offer the excitement for an evening on the town.

Based on a bag she purchased years ago in London, Sharon Commins designed **Sunset Aria** (first from left, front row). Because there was no tag, she is unable to credit the designer or manufacturer. Sharon just loved the squashy design, thinking it would make an ideal opera bag. Copying the design, she dye-painted everything for this project, including the rayon and cotton cording and the rose and leaves. Metallic thread couching in swirling shapes offer the perfect accent to this elegant bag.

Beth Schwartz Wheeler.

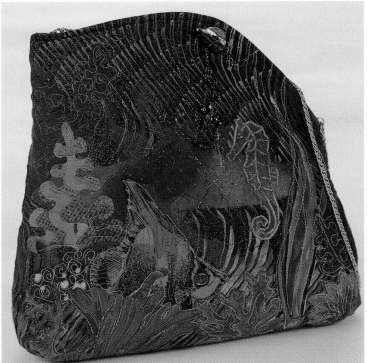

A closer look at both sides of the Carole Nicholas bag shows the sea horse created from three layers of tulle on one side, and a Portuguese Man-of-War, a fascinating floating creature with deadly stinging tentacles, on the other side. Free-motion metallic stitching accents the fish, seaweed, and other flora on the ocean floor. The folded purse takes the appearance of a shell floating with fish swimming by. A shell button with beads dangling from decorative threads gives the illusion of seaweed as a closure. Carole pivoted the clutch pattern to have a larger surface area to embellish.

Carole Nicholas.

Ruth Reynolds of Illinois believes that the best dressed people in this world are the kids on the street. They have no money to buy so-called fashion, so they are forced to hunt second-hand shops and attics for their clothes. In this way, they are forced to be creative and if you study them, you'll see that they certainly are. Ruth has created a line of clothing, Rivawear Ready-to-Wear. Her Riva character, known for her attitude, is one to truly tell it like it is. The sides of this mighty tote are graced with one of Riva's cartoons, making it an Official Riva Purse. "I just hate to change purses. I can't find anything for weeks." The important things like comb, brush, mirror, pen, sunglasses, and keys dangle from the outside of the bag, leaving plenty of room for other stuff in the roomy tote. Made for the Designer Showcase of Ghee's Challenge, Ruth says that this was great fun and she plans to use it when she lectures and teaches at guild meetings!

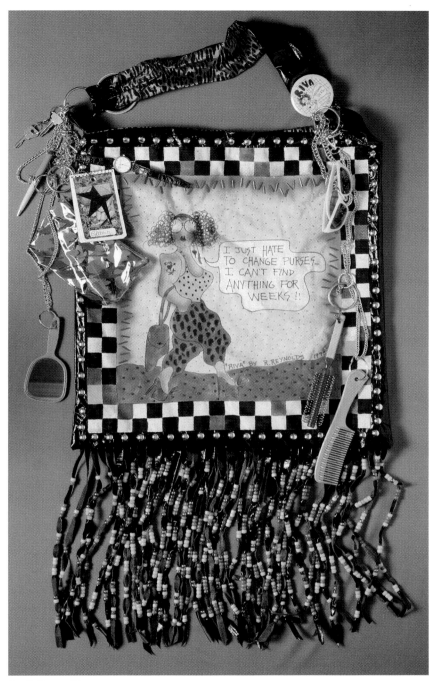

Ruth Reynolds.

Note: Most of the designers featured have books or patterns that are listed in Resources on page 123.

About the Author

Designer Linda McGehee is known worldwide for her award winning books, patterns, and spectacular techniques for manipulating fabrics. Her methods of texturizing and customizing fabrics to create unique surface textures and designs keep her constantly traveling to lecture at trade and consumer conventions, guilds, shops, and on television.

Her book, *Creating Texture With Textiles*, published by Krause Publications, shows many of her creations from the prestigious Fairfield Fashion Show, Statements, Capitol Imports, and *Better Homes & Gardens*. Her handbag and vest patterns are a palette to showcase these machine embellishments. Linda created 3-D designs for the embroidery machine through Cactus Punch. **Floral Dimensions** makes flowers come alive using various types of threads.

Resources

Avery, Virginia
Art-Wear: Only the best
Teacher • Designer • Author
731 King Street
Port Chester, NY 10573
(914) 939-3605

Bernadine's Needle Art
Punchneedle Kits • Thread • Supplies
PO Box 41
Arthur, IL 61911
(800) 884-8576 * Fax (217) 543-3019

Bossom, Diane
Author • Serge Art Teacher
http://www.sergerplace.com
E-mail: dbossom.sergeart@pdq.net

Butler, Jayne
Textile & Free-Motion Artist • Teacher
8377 Macawa Avenue
San Diego, CA 92123
(858) 565-4892
E-mail: jaynesew@aol.com

Carr, Anne
Teacher • Pattern Maker • Quilter
Zipped Up Tote Pattern
598 E Erie Street
Chandler, AZ 85225
(480) 963-4716

Caskey, Betty M.
Designer • Teacher • Seminar Organizer
Crazy Quilt Bridal Bag Pattern
Crazy Quilt Opera Purse Pattern
#1- 4610-45th Street
Olds, Alberta, Canada T4H 1A1
(888) 362-7455 * Fax (403) 556-1686
http://www.victorianpleasures.com
E-mail: silkworm@telusplanet.net

Commins, Sharon M.
Designer • Fiber Artist • Computer Artist
3630 Wade Street
Los Angeles, CA 90066
(310) 390-2644
E-mail: smcommins@email.msn.com

Fiber-Etch
Silkpaint Corporation
Products for Creative Solutions
PO Box 18
Waldron, MO 64092
(816) 891-7774 * Fax (816) 891-7775
http://www.silkpaint.com
E-mail: art@silkpaint.com

Four Corners Designs, Inc.
Innovative Books & Patterns
Cotton Chenille Purse Pattern
2115 Teakwood Suite 550
Plano, TX 75075
(800) 573-3687
http://www.fourcornersdesigns.com
E-mail: info@fourcornersdesigns.com

Ghee's
Handbag Patterns • Frames • Chains • Magnetic
  Snaps
2620 Centenary #2-250
Shreveport, LA 71104
(318) 226-1701 * Fax (318) 226-1781
http://www.ghees.com

Hester, Connie
Fiber Artist • Author • Instructor • Designer
Sling Bag/Purse Pattern
515 East 30th
Bryan, TX 77803
(409) 779-8113
http://members.aol.com/conhester/conniehester/
  intro.htm
E-mail: conhester@aol.com

Judy Bishop Designs
Artistic Clothing Designer • Instructor
24603 Island Avenue
Carson, CA 90745
(310) 835-6022

Kwilts & Kloze
Marty Lawrence
Surface Designer • Fiber Art Teacher
PO Box 4602
Flint, MI 48504

Liebzeit, Carole
Quilt Teacher • Garment Designer
8674 Kenwood Road
Cincinnati, OH 45242

Linda Crone Creations
Machine Artist • Teacher • Pattern Designer
Plentiful Pockets Bag Pattern
4832 White Oak
Rockford, IL 61114
http://www.lindacronecreations.com
E-mail: lccreatns@aol.com

Luke-Boone, Ronke
Designer • Teacher
The Picnic Tote Pattern
PO Box 3276
Falls Church, VA 22043
(703) 448-3884 * Fax (703) 749-0470

Luke-Boone, Ronke continued
http://www.imall.com/stores/rlboone
http://www.africancrafts.com
E-mail: RLBoone@RLBoone.com

McGehee, Linda
Designer • Author • Teacher
2620 Centenary Blvd #2-250
Shreveport, LA 71104
(318) 226-1701 * Fax (318) 226-1781
http://www.ghees.com

Murphy, Anita
Quilt Maker • Instructor • Author • Lecturer
  • Judge
3546 Ironwood Drive
Kountze, TX 77625
(409) 246-2948

Nicholas, Carole A.
Contemporary Quilt Maker • Designer •
  Teacher
Specializing in Quilted Garments
Seminar Coordinator for Jinny Beyer
2813 Bree Hill Road
Oakton, VA 22124
(703) 620-0917 * Fax (703) 620-0917

Raymond, Jenny
Teacher • Lecturer • Designer of Wearables
817 23rd Street
Gothenburg, NE 69138
(308) 537-3594
E-mail: jennyraymond@alltel.net

Reynolds, Ruth
Artist • Teacher • Designer
Rivawear Ready-to-Wear
22527 South Bramble Hill
Joliet, IL 60436
(815) 729-2371

Rhodes, Donna
Teacher • Author • Fiber Artist
213 Yarmouth Road
Fern Park, FL 32730
(407) 339-3684
http://www.warpandwoof.com
E-mail: donna@iag.net

Roberts, Annrae
Fiber Artist • Creativity Coach • Editor
Annrae's Creative Options Inc.
5700 Jackson Loop
Rio Rancho, NM 87124
(505) 892-3957 * Fax (505) 896-7948
E-mail: annraer@aol.com

Sapienza, Sandra
Designer • Teacher
 • Sewing Conference Planner
Fish Purse Pattern
PO Box 331
Crownsville, MD 21032
http://www.needlearts-adventures.com
E-mail: sandra@annpolis.net

Sharon Hultgren Designs
Quilt Tool & Fabric Designer • Teacher
904 Ridge Haven Circle
Buffalo, MN 55313

Shirley Botsford, Inc.
Designer • Author • Innkeeper
Pouf of A Purse Pattern
PO Box 686
19 High Street
Beacon, NY 12508
(914) 831-6099

Snap Source, Inc., The
Snaps & Snap Attaching Tools
PO Box 99733
Troy, MI 48099
(800) 725-4600
http://www.snapsource.com

Stachowicz, Kathy
Teacher • Pattern Designer • Author
1418 Meadowlark Street
Longwood, FL 32750
(407) 260-6680
E-mail: katstac@earthlink.net

Stephanie Kimura Designs
Pattern Designer • Teacher • Fiber Artist
PO Box 1471
Jensen Beach, FL 34958
(561) 286-8231
http://www.kimurapatterns.com

Susan Deal Design Studio
Fiber & Wearable Art • Teacher
1455 Bend Road
Prescott, AZ 86305
(520) 445-2697
E-mail: sddeal@primnet.com

Victorian Pleasures
Silk Ribbon Embroidery • Bias Cut & Wire Edge
 Ribbon
Crazy Quilt Fabrics • Threads • Beads • Books
 • Videos
#1-4610-45th Street
Olds, Alberta, Canada T4H 1A1
(888) 362-7455 * Fax (403) 556-1686
http://www.victorianpleasures.com
E-mail: silkworm@telusplanet.net

Wall, Ann
Pattern Designer
Fabulous Cutwork in Ultrasuede
3921 Fairwood Court
Midland, TX 79707
(915) 699-0375

Warp & Woof Creations
Surface Design for Fibre Artists
Patterns • Books • Supplies
PO Box 300121
Fernpark, FL 32730
(407) 339-3684 * Fax (407) 339-3471
www.warpandwoof.com

Wheeler, Beth
Publisher • Designer • Wearable Art
9165 Laurelwood Court
Manassas, VA 20110
E-mail: 14k@prodigy.net

Wilman, Michelle
Pattern Designer • Teacher • Button Collector
Triangulation Purse Pattern
Mamamania-Vintage Buttons
618 18th Ave. NW
Calgary, Alberta, Canada T2M 0T8
(403) 284-3266
www.mamamania.com

Index

Inspirational Designs Using Basic Techniques

Creating Texture with Textiles!
by Linda McGehee

Written for all levels of sewers, this user-friendly guide features step-by-step instructions to create spectacular one-of-a-kind designs on fabric with the use of any sewing machine. Techniques include piecing, spiraling, applique, piping, cording, embroidery, beading, among others.

Softcover • 8-1/4 x 10-7/8 • 128 pages
200 color photos & 20 illustrations
TWT • $21.95

Serge Art
Wearable Art for the Creative Serger
by Diane Bossom

Fully illustrated step-by-step instructions and color photos guide you to create more than a dozen wearable projects, including vests, jackets, and coats with any type of serger in two, three, four, and five thread combinations.

Softcover • 8-1/4 x 10-7/8 • 144 pages
150 color photos and 100 illustrations
SAWA • $21.95

Daddy's Ties
by Shirley Botsford

Shirley Botsford unknots some creative ideas for Dad's old, unused ties. Learn to make great keepsakes and one-of-a-kind gifts. Complete patterns, step-by-step instructions, and full-color illustrations show you how to make quilts, picture frames, and dozens of other beautiful treasures.

Softcover • 8-1/4 x 10-7/8 • 96 pages
color throughout
DADTI • $16.95

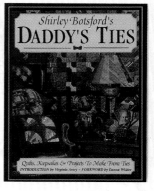

It's A Snap!
Secrets for Successful Snapping
by Jeanine Twigg

A simple and creative alternative to buttons and zippers, this book provides step-by-step methods for attaching snaps - on everything from infant wear to home decor. From basic snapping techniques to garment embellishment, children's games and even creative projects for those with special needs.

Softcover • 8-1/4 x 10-7/8 • 160 pages
100 color photos & 200 illustrations
SNAP • $19.95

Shirley Botsford's Decorating with Fabric Crafts
Elegant home accessory designs inspired by architectural elements
by Shirley Botsford

Learn how to make and display lovely fabric crafts in your home. Create complementary environments for the 25 simple, yet elegant, projects in this book that feature a variety of popular techniques such as quilting, ribbonwork, flower-making, and stenciling. Step-by-step instructions and helpful diagrams guide you.

Softcover • 8-1/4 x 10-7/8 • 128 pages
75 illustrations • 75 color photos
SBDEC • $21.95

Simple Techniques to Obtain a Fresh New Look

Fabric Landscapes by Machine

Decorative Stitching Styles for Quilted Scenes

by Linda Crone

Personalize any garment or home accessory with your favorite landscape. Stitch a wall hanging of that tranquil lake near your childhood home or add a dramatic mountain scene to a jacket. Noted landscape stitcher Linda Crone guides you through the process with quick and easy instructions - from basic supplies to decorative stitches to finishing touches. You'll learn to stitch landscapes on garments, tote bags and purses, pillows, greeting cards, wall hangings, and picture frames. Patterns for sample scenes are included.

Softcover • 8-1/4 x 10-7/8 • 128 pages
100 color photos
LDMA • $19.95

Celebrate the Seasons with Ribbon Embroidery by Machine

More Than 30 New Projects from the Authors of Ribbon Embroidery by Machine and More Ribbon Embroidery by Machine

by Marie Duncan and Betty Farrell

The masters of ribbon embroidery by machine have designed 30 great new projects relating to the seasons of the year. You'll learn new stitches and techniques to complete a wide variety of decorations and wearables. From an exquisite shawl to a simple ornament, crafters of all skill levels will be inspired to learn this fascinating technique using a sewing machine.

Softcover • 8-1/4 x 10-7/8 • 112 pages
100 color photos and 150 illustrations
SECR • $19.95

Ribbon Embroidery by Machine

by Marie Duncan and Betty Farrell

Your intricate, elegant embroidery can be trouble-free! Learn to use your sewing machine to create 25 basic stitches and 48 motifs with this easy-to-use book. Dress up jackets, photo frames, holiday ornaments, vests, and pillows with simple instructions for 11 projects.

Softcover • 8-1/4 x 10-7/8 • 96 pages
color throughout
REBM • $18.95

Treasured Wrappings

Fifteen of today's top designers have collaborated to present complete instructions for 45 unique and beautiful ways to package gifts. From Nancy Cornwell's Polarfleece® packages to Cari Clement's fabulously tasseled gift boxes, you'll find a treasure trove of easy, economical, and quick ways to make gift giving even more personal and meaningful.

Softcover • 8-1/4 x 10-7/8 • 128 pages
50 illustrations • 100 color photos
WRAP • $16.95

More Ribbon Embroidery by Machine

by Marie Duncan & Betty Farrell

Nineteen exciting projects using the popular ribbon embroidery by machine decorating method. Baby wearables to elegant evening bags are detailed in this instructional volume. Includes how to embellish ready-made items as well as techniques for incorporating beading and heirloom sewing.

Softcover • 8-1/4 x 10-7/8 • 96 pages
100 color photos
BCUR • $21.95